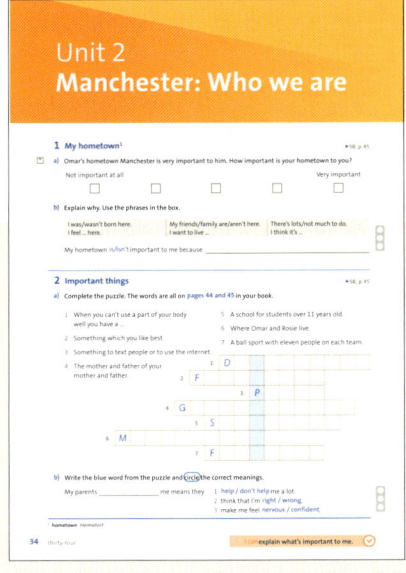 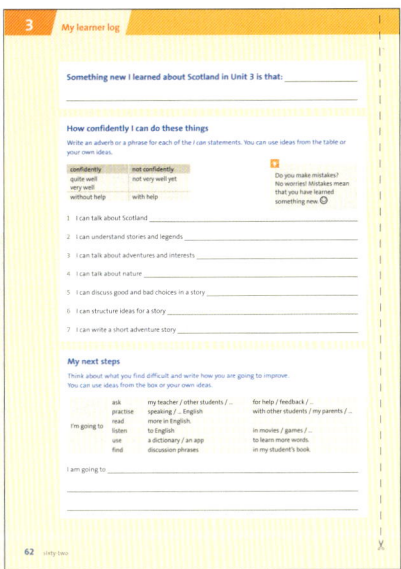 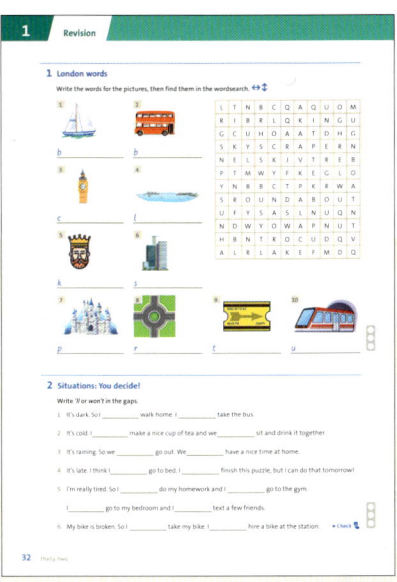

Wordpower

Auf diesen Seiten findest du Übungen zu den Vokabeln der jeweiligen Units und kannst dein gesprochenes Englisch verbessern.

My learner log

Hier kannst du auf die Unit zurückblicken und deinen Lernstand festhalten.

Revision

Halte auf diesen Seiten inne und wiederhole, was du in den vorherigen Units gelernt hast.

Dein Buch findest du auch in der Cornelsen Lernen App

Siehst du eines dieser Symbole in deinem Workbook, kannst du in deiner App …

alle Hörtexte und Videos zu deinem Arbeitsheft aufrufen.

▶ Digital help

auf Ideen und Hilfen zugreifen.

▶ Check

deine Antworten eigenständig überprüfen.

lighthouse 3

Workbook Lehrkräftefassung

Im Auftrag des Verlages erarbeitet von
Sydney Thorne, York; Zoe Thorne, Royston

In Zusammenarbeit mit der Englischredaktion
Klaus Unger (Projektleitung),
Karin Wedepohl (verantwortliche Redakteurin), Lisa Ahmadi,
Chiara Castellano, Michael Dunkel

Beratende Mitwirkung
Sabine Bay, Cloppenburg; Ulrike Plänker, Schmallenberg

Medienmanagement
Silke Kirchhoff

Illustrationen
Yaroslaw Schwarzstein, Hannover

Fotos
Anja Poehlmann, Brighton
Chocolate Films, London

Umschlaggestaltung
Rosendahl, Berlin

Layoutkonzept
Klein & Halm, Berlin

Layout und technische Umsetzung
PER MEDIEN & MARKETING GmbH, Braunschweig

Passend zum Workbook:
Sprechen, Aussprache, Wortschatz und Grammatik digital üben
mit der mobilen App ChatClass. Erhältlich auch als PrintPlus-Lizenz
bei Nutzung des Arbeitsheftes.

www.cornelsen.de

Soweit in diesem Lehrwerk Personen fotografisch abgebildet sind und ihnen von der Redaktion fiktive Namen, Berufe, Dialoge und Ähnliches zugeordnet oder diese Personen in bestimmte Kontexte gesetzt werden, dienen diese Zuordnungen und Darstellungen ausschließlich der Veranschaulichung und dem besseren Verständnis des Buchinhaltes.

Die Webseiten Dritter, deren Internetadressen in diesem Lehrwerk angegeben sind, wurden vor Drucklegung sorgfältig geprüft. Der Verlag übernimmt keine Gewähr für die Aktualität und den Inhalt dieser Seiten oder solcher, die mit ihnen verlinkt sind.

Dieses Werk berücksichtigt die Regeln der reformierten Rechtschreibung und Zeichensetzung.

Alle Drucke dieser Auflage sind inhaltlich unverändert und können im Unterricht nebeneinander verwendet werden.

© 2024 Cornelsen Verlag GmbH, Berlin

Das Werk und seine Teile sind urheberrechtlich geschützt. Jede Nutzung in anderen als den gesetzlich zugelassenen Fällen bedarf der vorherigen schriftlichen Einwilligung des Verlages. Hinweis zu §§ 60 a, 60 b UrhG: Weder das Werk noch seine Teile dürfen ohne eine solche Einwilligung an Schulen oder in Unterrichts- und Lehrmedien (§ 60 b Abs. 3 UrhG) vervielfältigt, insbesondere kopiert oder eingescannt, verbreitet oder in ein Netzwerk eingestellt oder sonst öffentlich zugänglich gemacht oder wiedergegeben werden. Dies gilt auch für Intranets von Schulen Schulen und anderen Bildungseinrichtungen.

Druck: ppm Fulda GmbH & Co. KG, Fulda

1. Auflage, 1. Druck 2024	1. Auflage, 1. Druck 2024
Workbook 3	Workbook 3 Lehrkräftefassung
ISBN 978-3-06-034600-4	ISBN 978-3-06-034597-7

PEFC-zertifiziert
Dieses Produkt stammt aus nachhaltig bewirtschafteten Wäldern, Recycling und kontrollierten Quellen

PEFC/04-31-1308 www.pefc.de

lighthouse 3 BASIC

Workbook Lehrkräftefassung

 Audios online verfügbar unter go.cornelsen.de **Code:** rovaru

 Dein Workbook findest du auch in der **Cornelsen Lernen App**.
Siehst du eines dieser Symbole in deinem Workbook, findest du in der App …

 alle **Audios**

 alle **Videos** und **Erklärfilme**

 Hilfen und **Lösungen** zu ausgewählten Aufgaben

Cornelsen

Quellenverzeichnis

Cover
Cornelsen/li.: Shutterstock.com/Ron Ellis/courtesy of Transport for London; Personen: Chocolate Films; Hintergrund re.: stock.adobe.com/anatoliycherkas

Illustrationen
Cornelsen/Yaroslav Schwarzstein: **S. 38/o.r.**, **S. 58**, **S. 64**, **S. 71**; Cornelsen/Yaroslaw Schwarzstein: **S. 20/u.r.**, **S. 23**, **S. 26/o.r.**, **S. 40/o.r.**, **S. 50**, **S. 52**, **S. 53**, **S. 57/u.**, **S. 58**, **S. 58/u.**, **S. 71**, **S. 74**, **S. 80**, **S. 89**.

Fotos
S. 2/m.: PEFC Deutschland e.V.; **S. 3/u.l.:** Cornelsen/Inhouse/Anne Weingarten; **S. 5/1:** Shutterstock.com/S-F; **S. 5/2:** stock.adobe.com/Kaspars; **S. 5/3:** Shutterstock.com/Fotimageon; **S. 5/4:** stock.adobe.com/Tomas Marek; **S. 5/5:** Shutterstock.com/John McGreevy; **S. 7/1:** stock.adobe.com/kelvn; **S. 7/2:** Imago Stock & People GmbH/Design Pics; **S. 7/3:** Imago Stock & People GmbH/Zoonar; **S. 7/4:** Imago Stock & People GmbH/Design Pics; **S. 7/5:** stock.adobe.com/Prostock-studio; **S. 7/6:** stock.adobe.com/Pixel-Shot; **S. 7/u.r.:** stock.adobe.com/jelenaaloskina; **S. 7/m.:** Cornelsen/Inhouse; **S. 8/A:** Imago Stock & People GmbH/Tom Mackie/Avalon.red; **S. 8/B:** Imago Stock & People GmbH/Zoonar; **S. 8**/C: Imago Stock & People GmbH/imago images/agefotostock/BuildPix/Photoshot; **S. 9:** Cornelsen/Anja Poehlmann; **S. 10/m.r.:** Cornelsen/Anja Poehlmann; **S. 10/o.r.:** Shutterstock.com/Tsekhmister; **S. 11/o.r.:** Cornelsen/Anja Poehlmann; **S. 11**/1-6: Cornelsen/Inhouse; **S. 12**/Herz: Shutterstock.com/JosepPerianes; **S. 12/o.l.**, o.r.: Cornelsen/Anja Poehlmann; **S. 12**/Icons: Cornelsen/Inhouse; **S. 14/m.r.:** stock.adobe.com/Mix and Match Studio; **S. 14/m.r.:** stock.adobe.com/stockyimages; **S. 14/o.l.:** Cornelsen/Inhouse; **S. 16**: stock.adobe.com/Eli Bolyarska; **S. 20/o.r.:** Shutterstock.com/Rocketclips, Inc.; **S. 21/A:** Shutterstock.com/QQ7; **S. 21/B:** stock.adobe.com/Bonsai Multimedia/chbaum; **S. 21/C:** mauritius images/alamy stock photo/Mickey Lee; **S. 21/D:** stock.adobe.com/elena; **S. 21/E:** stock.adobe.com/marcorubino; **S. 21/F:** Imago Stock & People GmbH/agefotostock/claudiodivizi; **S. 21/u.r.:** stock.adobe.com/Andrew Barker; **S. 22/m.r.:** Imago Stock & People GmbH/imagebroker/Mara Brandl; **S. 22/o.r.:** Cornelsen/Chocolate Films; **S. 24/u.r.:** Imago Stock & People GmbH/Addictive Stock/David Fuentes; **S. 25:** Shutterstock.com/Pixel-Shot; **S. 26/m.r.:** stock.adobe.com/Wigandt; **S. 27:** Digital Learning Ass. Ltd.; **S. 28/1:** Shutterstock.com/Olhastock; **S. 28/10:** Shutterstock.com/titov dmitriy; **S. 28/2:** Shutterstock.com/grey_and; **S. 28/5:** Shutterstock.com/Olesia Bech; **S. 28/8:** Shutterstock.com/Maks Narodenko; **S. 28/9:** Shutterstock.com/MaraZe; **S. 28/u.r.:** Shutterstock.com/unguryanu; **S. 29:** stock.adobe.com/binik; **S. 31:** stock.adobe.com/yurolaitsalbert; **S. 32/1:** stock.adobe.com/topvectors; **S. 32/10:** Shutterstock.com/Boyko.Pictures; **S. 32/2:** mauritius images/Tomacco/Alamy Stock Photos; **S. 32/3:** Shutterstock.com/RedlineVector; **S. 32/4:** Shutterstock.com/Oceloti; **S. 32/5:** stock.adobe.com/mr_marcom; **S. 32/6:** Shutterstock.com/Iconic Bestiary; **S. 32/7:** stock.adobe.com/Zaharia Levy; **S. 32/8:** mauritius images/Maximilian Laschon/Alamy Stock Photos; **S. 32/9:** mauritius images/YAY Media AS/Alamy Stock Photos; **S. 33:** Shutterstock.com/ArtMari; **S. 35/1:** Imago Stock & People GmbH/Addictive Stock/Franci Leoncio; **S. 35/2:** mauritius images/Cavan Images; **S. 35/3:** Imago Stock & People GmbH/Addictive Stock/CienXCien Studio; **S. 36:** Shutterstock.com/HollyHarry; **S. 37:** Shutterstock.com/siamionau pavel; **S. 38/u.r.:** Shutterstock.com/oliveromg; **S. 39:** Shutterstock.com/SynthEx; **S. 40/u.r.:** Imago Stock & People GmbH/Addictive Stock/Franci Leoncio; **S. 41:** Imago Sportfotodienst GmbH/PA Images; **S. 42:** stock.adobe.com/guas; **S. 43:** Cornelsen/Chocolate Films; **S. 45:** stock.adobe.com/contrastwerkstatt; **S. 46:** stock.adobe.com/Icons-Studio; **S. 48/1:** Shutterstock.com/Zenmind; **S. 48/2:** Shutterstock.com/Olga 777; **S. 48/3:** Shutterstock.com/PinkPueblo; **S. 48/4:** Shutterstock.com/Nsit; **S. 48/5:** Shutterstock.com/Veniamin Kraskov; **S. 48/6:** Shutterstock.com/Just Dzine; **S. 51**: Shutterstock.com/Panda Vector; **S. 55:** Imago Stock & People GmbH/imago/Westend61; **S. 57/o.:** Shutterstock.com/AlyonaZhitnaya; **S. 58/o.r.:** Imago Stock & People GmbH/Wirestock; **S. 59:** Digital Learning Ass. Ltd.; **S. 61:** stock.adobe.com/CleverStock; **S. 65/m.r.:** mauritius images/George Mutch/Alamy/Alamy Stock Photos; **S. 65/u.r.:** Imago Stock & People GmbH/Shotshop; **S. 66/1:** Shutterstock.com/FGraphix; **S. 66/**2: Shutterstock.com/Lana Nikova; **S. 66/3:** Shutterstock.com/Giuseppe_R; **S. 66/4:** Shutterstock.com/vandemakou; **S. 66/Deutschland Flagge:** shutterstock.com/Paul Stringer; **S. 66/m.r.:** Shutterstock.com/Peter Hermes Furian; **S. 66/Uk Flagge:** stock.adobe.com/stock.adobe.com/Visual Content; **S. 67/1:** stock.adobe.com/dudlajzov; **S. 67/2:** stock.adobe.com/mtrommer; **S. 67/3:** mauritius images/TinasDreamworld/Alamy Stock Photos; **S. 67/4:** stock.adobe.com/tinasdreamworld; **S. 67/5:** Imago Stock & People GmbH; **S. 68**: stock.adobe.com/New Africa; **S. 69**: Imago Stock & People GmbH/imago images/MASKOT; **S. 70/m.r.:** Depositphotos/Abhishek Rastogi; **S. 70/m.r.:** stock.adobe.com/Bhaven; **S. 72/m.l.:** Shutterstock.com/Ebtikar; **S. 72/o.l.:** Depositphotos/XAVIER LORENZO; **S. 72/u.l.:** stock.adobe.com/Sangiao_Photography; **S. 73/u.r.:** Shutterstock.com/AYO Production; **S. 79**/o.l.: Shutterstock.com/Maksim Denisenko; **S. 79/u.r.:** Cornelsen/Chocolate Films; **S. 81:** Cornelsen/Chocolate Films; **S. 82:** Imago Stock & People GmbH/robertharding; **S. 83/m.r.:** Shutterstock.com/Ariya J; **S. 83/o.r.:** stock.adobe.com/Ruth P. Peterkin; **S. 84:** stock.adobe.com/worldwide_stock; **S. 86:** akg-images/UIG/Universal History Archive; **S. 90/m.r.:** Imago Stock & People GmbH/Loop Images/Highwaystarz.

Inhalt

	So lernst du mit Lighthouse	U2
	Impressum	2
	Quellenverzeichnis	4
	Inhaltsverzeichnis	5
	Check-up: Ermittlung der Lernausgangslage	6

Hello!
Where we're from — 16

Unit 1
London: City life — 18

Revision 1 — 32

Unit 2
Manchester: Who we are — 34

Revision 2 — 48

Unit 3
Scotland: Adventure — 50

Revision 3 — 64

Unit 4
Wales: Digital life — 66

Revision 4 — 80

Unit 5
Two Irelands: Together — 82

Partner pages — 89

Typical tasks — 92

five **5**

Check-up — Vocabulary

1 Opposites

Match the adjectives 1–6 with their opposites a–g.

| a boring | b late | c messy | d nervous | e noisy | f slow |

1 fast — **f**   2 interesting — **a**   3 tidy — **c**
4 confident — **d**   5 quiet — **e**   6 early — **b**

▶ Check ____ / 6

Die Check-up-Seiten können zur Ermittlung der Lernausgangslage genutzt werden.

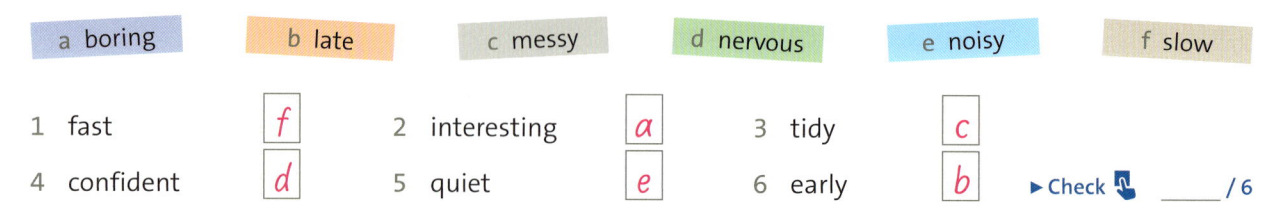

2 Find the verb

Write a verb that can fit with each group of words.

do • get • go • listen • play • watch

1 *play* — tennis / computer games / the guitar
2 *go* — to the cinema / into town / to the beach / on holiday / shopping
3 *listen* — to music / to the teacher / to a podcast
4 *watch* — TV / a film / a video / a football match
5 *do* — your homework / yoga / the washing / a puzzle
6 *get* — on a train / up / pocket money / wet

▶ Check ____ / 6

3 Odd word out

Which word doesn't fit? Write why. Use the words in the box. You get one point for each right odd word out and one point for each correct explanation.

family member • ~~negative word~~ • room • sport • subject • vegetable

1 excited   kind   unfriendly   helpful
   Unfriendly doesn't fit because it's *a negative word.*

2 swimming   cooking   trampolining   football
   Cooking doesn't fit because it's *not a sport.*

3 friend   brother   cousin   stepmother
   Friend doesn't fit because it's *not a family member.*

4 chicken   sausage   ham   potato
   Potato doesn't fit because it's *a vegetable.*

5 bed   toilet   wardrobe   chair
   Toilet doesn't fit because it's *a room.*

6 maths   English   geography   classroom
   Classroom doesn't fit because it's *not a subject.*

▶ Check ____ / 10

Check-up Listening

4 Chloe's morning

Listen to Lily's sister Chloe talking about her mornings and complete the clocks.

07:30

07:45

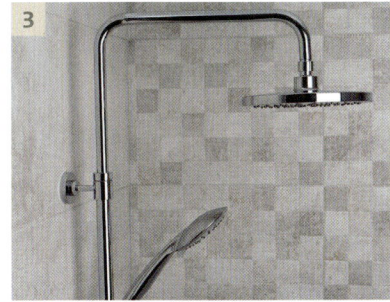
08:00

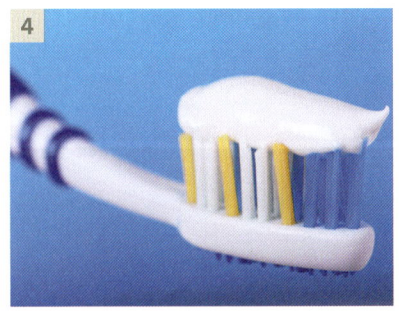
08:20

08:25

08:45

▶ Check _____ / 5

5 Meeting Dario

a) Listen to the conversation. What kind of conversation is it? Tick (✓) the right box.

1 a job interview ✓   2 a phone call ☐   3 a dialogue at school ☐   4 a podcast ☐

b) Listen again and (circle) the correct answers.

1 Dario wants to be a (babysitter) / cleaner.
2 Dario has never done this job before / (has done this job a lot).
3 Dario is (13) / 14 years old.
4 Dario is never hard-working / (late).
5 Dario maybe wants to be a (teacher) / cricket player one day.
6 Dario (doesn't want the job) / (gets the job).

▶ Check _____ / 7

Check-up — Reading

6 Which home?

Match the photos (A–C) to the adverts (1–3). Write the letter in the box.

1 FOR SALE[1]: Modern flat with two bedrooms and one bathroom on the fourth floor in the town centre. **B**

2 FOR SALE: Small, quiet house with a garden in the country. Ground floor only. **C**

3 FOR SALE: Big, traditional house with two floors and four bedrooms. Small garden with trees. **A**

▶ Check _____ / 3

7 Our chores

Read the three messages and the seven sentences.
Write if each sentence is about PizzaFan55 (P), SurferGirl (S) or BookWorm42 (B).

PizzaFan55 What chores do you have to do, everyone? I think my dad is so mean because I have to help SO much at home. I have to set the table for dinner every night AND then empty the dishwasher. I also have to take out the rubbish every week.. It's not fair!

SurferGirl Oh, that's a lot! I'm lucky – I don't have to do many chores. I have to tidy my room sometimes, of course, and I babysit my little sister every four weeks. But that's it! I'm happy that I don't have to take out the rubbish or clean the bathroom – yuck!

BookWorm42 I don't have to do any chores if I don't want to, but my parents give me money when I help at home. For example, when I vacuum the floors, I get £3. I think that's a great idea and that way, everyone is happy.

1 This person isn't happy with their chores. **P**
2 This person doesn't have to help at home. **B**
3 This person has to do a chore every day. **P**
4 This person has to look after someone. **S**
5 This person has to tidy their room. **S**
6 This person sometimes does extra chores. **B**
7 This person has to take out the rubbish. **P**

▶ Check _____ / 6

[1] **for sale** zu verkaufen

Check-up — Reading

8 Finn's holiday

Read Finn's email to Sunita and say if the sentences are true (T) or false (F).

---

to: Sunita
from: Finn

Hey Sunita

How are you? Did you have a nice holiday?

We've just returned from holiday. Normally we go to Usedom in the north of Germany, and we stay in a holiday house by the beach there. It's fun, but the weather can be cold and windy – that's not so good!!

So it was great that we did something a bit different this year. We went to Turkey to visit my dad's family, and we stayed with my aunt and uncle in Istanbul. It's an amazing city – you'd love it! I went there when I was really little, but I didn't remember it, of course.

It's a bit different to most cities because it's on two continents[1]. My aunt and uncle live on the east side of the river, in Asia, but we often went to the west side by boat. So we saw a lot of sights in Europe! We visited lots of beautiful mosques and the biggest market in the world! I bought a present for my friend Suri, but we didn't buy any spices because my aunt likes those in the market near her house better.

It was Ramadan when we were there, so we didn't eat or drink during the day. But most evenings, we went to a big park called Sultanahmet Square, where lots of people had picnics and music to celebrate the end of the fast. People sold all kinds of food and drink, but my favourite was the apple tea!

What did you do during the holidays? It was your first holiday together with Ben and Willow too, right?

Write to me soon and tell me everything!

Finn

---

1 Finn went to Germany this year. **F**
2 He doesn't like the weather on his normal holiday. **T**
3 He stayed in a holiday home in Turkey. **F**
4 It was his first time in Istanbul. **F**
5 He sometimes went to the other side of the city by boat. **T**
6 He bought spices for his friend in the big market. **F**
7 He ate evening meals outside with other people. **T**
8 He really liked a hot drink. **T**

▶ Check ____ / 8

---

[1] **continent** *der Kontinent*

Check-up Grammar

9 Coding Robbie

a) Write the three regular verbs in the simple past.

! Irregular verbs have a special form.

1. work: Yesterday I *worked* harder.
2. live: When I was younger we *lived* in Turkey.
3. try: Yesterday I *tried* to run 5 km.

b) Complete the text with the verbs in the simple past. Remember that some verbs are irregular!

Yesterday, there (1) *was* (be) a new pet in Sunita's home —

— a sick baby cat!

Sunita (2) *liked* (like) the baby cat and she (3) *played*

(play) with it all afternoon. She (4) *gave* (give) it some milk and she

(5) *put* (put) the baby cat in her bed. But it

(6) *got up* (get up) a lot in the night and (7) *tried* (try) to jump on all the beds, so

they (8) *were* (be) all very tired the next day! And they (9) *weren't* (not be) happy!

c) Sunita asked Robbie some questions to test her code. Look at the highlighted verbs in Robbie's answers. Use them to complete the questions in the simple past.

1. What *did* you *eat* for breakfast this morning?
   — I'm a robot, so I didn't eat any breakfast!

2. How *did* you *help* me yesterday?
   — I helped you with your homework.

3. Where *did* Sunita *put* the baby cat last night?
   — She put it in her bed.

4. *Did* Finn *write* me a message today? — Yes, he wrote you a message.

5. What *was* the weather like yesterday? — It was cold but sunny.

6. *Did* you *take* the chocolate in my room? — No, Nish took it, not me!

▶ Check ____ / 17

Check-up   Grammar

10 An interview with Jodie

Jodie is one of the head students at Varndean School.
Complete the interview with verbs in the simple present.

Raj   Hi Jodie! What year (1) *are* (be) you in?

Jodie I (2) *'m* (be) in Year 11.

Raj   What (3) *'s* (be) your favourite subject and why?

Jodie I (4) *love* (love) design and technology because the teacher (5) *is* (be) nice. Also, my dad (6) *has* (have) a garage and I (7) *want* (want) to be a mechanic like him one day.

Raj   What do you (8) *do* (do) in your free time?

Jodie Sometimes I (9) *go* (go) to the gym¹ or I (10) *sing* (sing) in the school choir². Or I (11) *meet* (meet) my friends and we all sit and (12) *watch* (watch) funny videos together. My best friend (13) *does* (do) street dance every week, so she often (14) *makes* (make) her own cool dance videos. But not me (15) – I *don't dance* (not dance) ever!

▶ Check ____ / 14

11 Weather forecast

Look at the weather symbols and complete the sentences. Use the will-future + the right weather words.

It *'ll be sunny* in the north.

It *'ll be rainy* in the west.

It *'ll be windy* in the south.

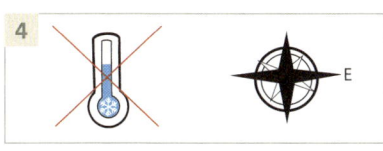

It *won't be cold* in the east.

It *'ll be snowy* in the mountains.

It *won't rain* at the beach.

▶ Check ____ / 5

---

¹ **gym** *das Fitnessstudio*   ² **school choir** *der Schulchor*

Check-up Speaking

12 An invitation

Zane is inviting Lily to a party. Partner A is Zane and Partner B is Lily. Act the conversation with a partner. Use the pictures to help you. You get one point for every correct sentence.

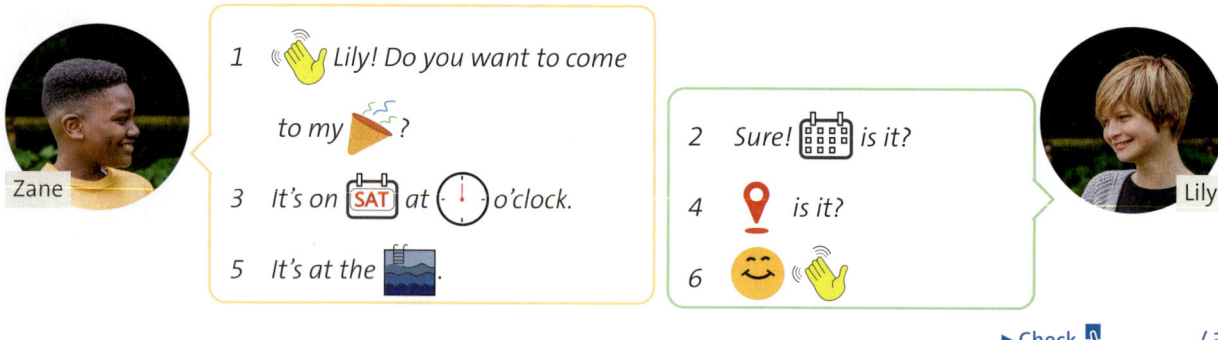

1 Lily! Do you want to come to my 🎉 ?
2 Sure! 📅 is it?
3 It's on [SAT] at ⏰ o'clock.
4 📍 is it?
5 It's at the 🏊.
6 😊 👋

▶ Check ____ / 3

13 My school life

a) Use the information below to give a one-minute talk about your school life. Make notes. You can record your talk.

Remember to …	Points
1 name your two favourite places in school: *My favourite places are …*	___ / 2
2 name two subjects you like. *My favourite subjects are …*	___ / 2
3 name one subject you don't like. *I don't like …*	___ / 1
4 say what you did at school yesterday. (Use the simple past!) *Yesterday I …*	___ / 2
5 speak slowly.	___ / 1
6 speak clearly.	___ / 1

My favourite places are

My favourite subjects are

I don't like

Yesterday I

b) Present your talk to a partner or give them your recording. Your partner gives feedback in the table in a).

▶ Check ____ / 9

Check-up — Writing

14 My favourite character

a) Write a description of your favourite character from a book, film, series or game. Use the information 1–5 in the brown list below. First make notes.

(Harry Potter, eleven years old, black hair, round glasses, old clothes, uniform, student, magic, brave)

Remember to ...	Points
1 say three things about the character (age, where they live, what they do, ...).	___ / 3
2 use adjectives to describe what the character looks like (tall, beautiful, cool, dangerous, ...).	___ / 1
3 describe what the character wears (glasses, helmet, mask, cape, ...).	___ / 1
4 use adjectives to describe the character (brave, clever, strong, funny, confident, fair, honest, ...).	___ / 1
5 say why you like that character.	___ / 1

b) Now write your text. Write about 40–60 words.

My favourite character is *(Harry Potter!*

In the first book he is eleven years old.

He has messy black hair and round glasses.

Harry wears old clothes from his cousin or his school uniform because he's a student at Hogwart's.

He's really brave and he likes adventures.

I like him because he can do magic.)

► Check ___ / 7

Check-up — Mediation

15 A lost pet

Read the poster for a lost pet and explain it in German. Find out: What happened? What does the pet look like? What does the pet do? What should you do? Give yourself a point for each piece of information.

Can you help? Our dog **Bingo** ran away yesterday. He is big but very friendly, and he's **black and white**. He loves running after a ball and he will come to you if you call him. If you see him, please text this number!
07700 900426

Gestern ist ein großer, schwarz-weißer und lieber Hund namens Bingo entlaufen. Er spielt gerne mit dem Ball und hört auf seinen Namen. Falls ihn jemand sieht, dann bitte unter der angegebenen Nummer melden.

▶ Check ____ / 4

16 In the restaurant

You are in a restaurant in Brighton with your grandmother, who doesn't speak English.
Write what you will say to each person below.

Waiter Hello, what would you like to order?
YOU *Was möchtest du bestellen?* (1 point)

Grandma Was für vegetarisches Essen haben sie?
YOU *What vegetarian food do you have?* (1 point)

Waiter We have a pizza with cheese and tomato or a veggie burger with chips.
YOU *Pizza mit Käse und Tomaten oder einen Veggieburger mit Pommes.* (1 point)

Grandma Dann nehme ich den Veggieburger mit Salat, bitte.
YOU *A veggie burger with a salad, please.* (1 point)

Waiter And what would you like to drink?
YOU *Und was magst du trinken?* (1 point)

Grandma Eine Cola, bitte.
YOU *A cola, please.* (1 point)

Waiter Of course.

▶ Check ____ / 6

Check-up — Evaluation

Evaluating[1] my skills

Complete the table with your points from pages 6–14. Then colour the traffic lights.

Skill	Points				Evaluation	Übungsmaterial
Vocabulary	**1** ☐ +	**2** ☐ +	**3** ☐	= total ☐	17–22 = green 12–16 = orange 11 or under = red	Check-up: Vocabulary 1 Check-up: Vocabulary 2 Check-up: Vocabulary 3 Check-up: Vocabulary 4
Listening	**4** ☐ +	**5** ☐		= total ☐	10–12 = green 6–9 = orange 5 or under = red	Check-up: Listening 1 Check-up: Listening 2 Check-up: Listening 3 Check-up: Listening 4
Reading	**6** ☐ +	**7** ☐ +	**8** ☐	= total ☐	14–17 = green 9–13 = orange 8 or under = red	Check-up: Reading 1 Check-up: Reading 2 Check-up: Reading 3 Check-up: Reading 4 Check-up: Reading 5
Grammar	**9** ☐ +	**10** ☐ +	**11** ☐	= total ☐	28–36 = green 19–27 = orange 18 or under = red	Check-up: Grammar 1 Check-up: Grammar 2 Check-up: Grammar 3 Check-up: Grammar 4 Check-up: Grammar 5 Check-up: Grammar 6
Speaking	**12** ☐ +	**13** ☐		= total ☐	10–12 = green 6–9 = orange 5 or under = red	Check-up: Speaking 1 Check-up: Speaking 2 Check-up: Speaking 3
Writing	**14** ☐				6–7 = green 4–5 = orange 3 or under = red	Check-up: Writing 1 Check-up: Writing 2 Check-up: Writing 3 Check-up: Mediation 1 Check-up: Mediation 2
Mediation	**15** ☐ +	**16** ☐		= total ☐	9–10 = green 6–8 = orange 5 or under = red	

Nachdem die Lernausgangslage mit dem *Check-up* ermittelt wurde, können die Schülerinnen und Schüler individuell mit dem Übungsmaterial gefördert und gefordert werden. Das Übungsmaterial besteht aus Kopiervorlagen auf bis zu vier Niveaustufen:

- ☐ Förder-Niveau
- ☒ einfaches Niveau
- ☒ mittleres Niveau
- ☒ hohes/forderndes Niveau

Die Rückseiten der Kopiervorlagen sind zur Selbstkontrolle mit den Lösungen versehen. Für *Speaking*- und *Writing*-Aufgaben, die den Erfahrungshorizont der Schülerinnen und Schüler einbeziehen und somit sehr individuell gelöst werden, gibt es zum Teil Musterlösungen. Hier sind aber auch Sie als Feedback-Instanz gefragt.
Zusammengestellt wurde dieses Übungsmaterial aus dem Material Extra-Differenzierung zu *Lighthouse* Band 1 und 2. Sie finden die Kopiervorlagen im *Unterrichtsmanager Plus* zu Band 3 von *Lighthouse*.

---

[1] (to) **evaluate sth.** *etw. beurteilen, etw. einschätzen*

Hello!
Where we're from

1 READING Places in the book
▶ Digital help   ▶ SB, p. 13

Read the photo descriptions and find the photos in your book. Write the page number for each one.

1. This is a photo of Conwy Castle in North Wales. The sky is blue and in the foreground there's a white bridge over the river. (Hello!) *page 13*

2. This is a photo of St James's Park in the middle of London. In the foreground, there's a large lake with four white birds near it. (Unit 1) *page 20*

3. This is a photo of Manchester in the north-west of England. It's a small photo, but you can see a park, and lots of tall buildings in the background. (Unit 2) *page 45*

4. This is a photo of a street in Edinburgh, the capital of Scotland. You can see a tall church and, on the right of the picture, some red phone boxes. (Unit 3) *page 73*

5. This is a photo of a beach in Wales. On the left of the picture, you can see some people. In the background there is a big white hotel. (Unit 4) *page 102*

6. In the foreground you can see a boat, but it isn't on water. In the background there is a big building: it is bigger at the top than at the bottom. (Unit 5) *page 132*

2 WRITING A photo description
▶ SB, p. 13

Look at the photo of another place in the UK, Inverness, and write a description like in exercise 1. Use the words and phrases in exercise 1 to help you:

> In the foreground you can see / there is / there are ...
> In the background I can see / there is / there are ...
> On the right / left of the picture ...
> You can see ...

This is a photo of Inverness. In the foreground there's a bridge. In the background you can see two churches. The sky is grey and cloudy.

Hello!

3 READING More UK cities ▶ SB, p. 13

Read the descriptions and write the cities on the map of the UK.

1 Aberdeen is a city in the north-east of Scotland.
2 Derry (sometimes called Londonderry) is a city in the north-west of Northern Ireland.
3 Norwich is a city in the east of England.
4 York is a city in the north-east of England. It is to the north of Norwich.
5 Newcastle is a city in the north of England, north of York.
6 Plymouth is a city next to the sea in the south-west of England.
7 Swansea is a city next to the sea in the south of Wales.
8 Brighton is a city in the south of England, next to the sea.

¹ **coast** *die Küste*

Unit 1
London: City life

1 Five photos of London
▶ SB, p. 15

Look again at pictures A–E on pages 14 and 15 in your English book. In which pictures can you see …

1 a street lamp? **A, B, C**
2 a cloud? **A, B, C, D, E**
3 a flag? **C, D**
4 a bridge? **B**
5 boats? **E**
6 a river? **B, E**
7 a car? **A**
8 windows? **A, B, C, D, E**
9 a clock? **B**
10 a tree? **A, B, D**
11 shops? **A**

Tip: There can be more than one answer.

2 London sights
▶ SB, p. 15

Write the words in the puzzle. All the words are on pages 14 and 15 of your book.

1 A tall part of a building.
2 The … family lives in Buckingham Palace.
3 The London Eye is a big …
4 An old, very strong building that helped to keep the people inside safe.
5 A very big house especially of a king or queen.
6 A great place for shopping and amazing food. *(two words)*
7 A famous clock. *(two words)*

Crossword answers:
1 **T**
2 **ROYAL**
3 **WHEEL**
4 **CASTLE**
5 **PALACE**
6 **CAMDEN MARKET**
7 **BIG BEN**

I can understand and share information about London.

Topic 1

3 On the tube
▶ SB, p. 16

Answer questions 1–5. Find the answers on the underground ticket and (circle) them.

1 How much does the ticket cost? **£ 0.85**

2 Where does the trip start? Where does it end? **King's Cross, Westminster**

3 Can you go back with the ticket?
No, you can't.

4 Can people who are older than 15 use this ticket?
No, they can't.

5 When can you travel with this tricket?
On Saturday 15th September

> Saturday 15th September   SINGLE
> From: King's Cross   To: Westminster
> 10–15 CHILD   £0.85

4 READING Journey puzzle
▶ SB, p. 16

a) Ali, Lily and Pearl are going to different places in London on Saturday. Read the sentences and look at the information in the bubbles. Then complete the table with the information from the bubbles.

1 Ali will cycle, but his journey will be the most expensive.
2 Lily won't go to a market, but she will take the tube.
3 Pearl will go to a train station, but she won't take the tube.
4 Pearl's journey won't cost anything.

> Arbeite nach dem Ausschlussverfahren und ergänze die Tabelle mit den Möglichkeiten, die übrig bleiben.

Victoria Station / Houses of Parliament / Camden Market

bus / city bike / underground

85p / £1.65 / free

	Where?	How?	How much?
Ali	Camden Market	city bike	£1.65
Lily	Houses of Parliament	underground	85p
Pearl	Victoria Station	bus	free

b) Look at the table again. Who will use the ticket in 3? **Lily**

5 MEDIATION Buying a ticket ▶ SB, p. 17

A German tourist asks you to help her buy a ticket in London.
Read what she wants to know and then complete questions 1–5.

Ach, du sprichst Englisch? Toll! Kannst du mir bitte helfen? Ich möchte wissen, …

1. *was eine Einzelfahrkarte nach Oxford Street kostet.*
2. *ob ich mit der Karte zahlen kann.*
3. *welche U-Bahn-Linie ich brauche.*
4. *ob ich umsteigen muss.*
5. *wann der nächste Zug fährt.*

1. How much is a single ticket for Oxford Street, _____ please?
2. Can I pay by card?
3. Which line is it? / do I need? / goes to Oxford Street?
4. Do I need to change?
5. When is the next train? does the next train go?

6 LANGUAGE Going to the station ▶ SB, p. 17

Lily is going away to visit her grandma. Complete the dialogue with *will/'ll* or *won't*.

Lily Bye bye then, Pearl. I'm on my way to Victoria Station.

Pearl _Will_ you hire a bike?

Lily I like cycling, but I _won't_ hire a bike this time because I have three big bags. I _'ll_ take the bus.

Pearl The tube is faster. Take the Northern Line and you _won't_ have to change trains.

Lily You're right. Thank you, I _'ll_ do that. Bye!

I can **talk about transport in London.**

Topic 2

7 LISTENING A tour of London ▶ SB, p. 18

a) Listen to the tour guide. What kind of tour is it? Circle the correct answer.

A Music Tour   (B) Ghost Tour   C Segway Tour

b) Listen again and tick the places that the people see on the tour.

☐ Buckingham Palace

☑ Houses of Parliament

☑ London Dungeon

☐ London Eye

☑ Shakespeare's Globe Theatre

☑ Tower of London

8 WRITING My dream tour of London ▶ Digital help   ▶ SB, p. 18

Complete the sentences about your dream tour of London.
Tip: Pages 14–18 in your book will give you ideas.

On my dream tour of London, I want to travel by _(segway / bike / taxi / …)_.

I want to visit _(Buckingham Palace_

because _the King lives there_

and I also want to see _the Tower of London_

because _it's scary and I like ghosts / …)_.

1 Topic 2

9 LANGUAGE What will Ali do? ▶ SB, p. 19

a) Read the sentences 1–6. Underline the simple present and circle the will-future.

1 If it <u>rains</u>, he'll travel by bus, but if <u>it's</u> sunny, he'll ride a city bike.
2 If he <u>travels</u> by bike, he'll have lunch in St James' Park.
3 If <u>it's</u> a Sunday, the museum won't be open.
4 If the museum <u>is</u> closed, he'll go to Camden Market with Pearl.
5 If he <u>sees</u> pelicans in St James' Park, he'll feed them.
6 If Ali and Pearl <u>go</u> to Camden Market, they'll buy lunch in the market.

b) Now read what really happened and answer the questions.
Tip: Read the sentences in 9a) very carefully. They will give you the answers.

On Sunday, it rained.

1 Where did Ali go? *To Camden Market with Pearl.*
2 How did he travel? *By bus.*
3 Where did he eat? *In the market.*

10 LANGUAGE London tips

a) Read sentences 1–6.
Underline the if-clauses.

b) Complete the sentences with the correct form of the verbs.

> **!**
> Remember:
> main clause: *will*-future;
> *if*-clause: simple present

1 The shops *won't be* (not be) too busy <u>if you visit London on a weekday</u>.
2 West End theatre tickets *will be* (be) cheaper <u>if you buy them on the day</u>.
3 You *will see* (see) all of London <u>if you go on the London Eye</u>.
4 <u>If you *buy*</u> (buy) tickets for the London Dungeon online, they will be cheaper.
5 <u>If you *wear*</u> (wear) the right shoes, your feet won't hurt.
6 <u>If you *walk*</u> (walk) too slowly in the street, London people won't be happy!!

11 Where will Lily go? ▶ SB, p. 21

a) Read the directions. If Lily follows them from Charing Cross Road, where will she finish?

1. Take the first road on the right, then go straight over the roundabout at Tower and Neal Street. This place is on the right. _theatre_

2. Go straight on and take the second road on the left. This place is on the left. _bank_

3. Turn right at the shops. Take the first left, then go straight over the second roundabout. This place is on the right. _hospital_

4. Go straight on and turn right at the sports centre. Go straight on past the school, then turn left at the roundabout. This place is on the right. _library_

b) Write directions for Lily to get to Charles Road station. ▶ Digital help

(Go straight on and turn right at the sports centre. Go straight on past the school. Go over the roundabout and it's on your right. / …)

c) Your partner plays Lily. You give directions to a place on the map. Does Lily finish at the correct place? Then swap roles.

I can **plan a tour.**

1 Topic 3

12 SPEAKING What's on the menu?   ▶ SB, p. 23

Lily and Pearl visit another cafe in London but there's a problem with the menus.
Work with a partner.
Partner B: Look at page 89.
Partner A: Ask your partner for the missing information and complete your menu.

How much is/are …?   *What costs £ …?*   *What's in a …?*

Greg's Breakfast Cafe

Big English breakfast (bacon[1], eggs, sausage, mushrooms[2], baked beans)	£7.50	Turkish breakfast (*bread*, hummus, *cucumber*, *eggs*, tomatoes)	£6.50
Vegetarian English breakfast (*eggs*, mushrooms, *tomatoes*, baked beans)	£6.25	Muesli with milk or yoghurt	£2.25
		Fruit salad	£2.75
Eggs on toast	£3.50	Tea or coffee	£1.75
Pancakes	£3.25	Fruit juice	£1.50
Toast with butter and *jam*	£2.00	Sparkling water	£1.50

13 LISTENING Pearl and Brianna's weekend   ▶ SB, p. 23

🔊 04

a) Pearl's little sister Brianna is talking to her grandma on the phone. Listen and (circle) the correct answer.

1 Pearl and Brianna had a visit from their …   P friends.   (M) family.   L grandma.
2 In Trafalgar Square, they saw …   (E) musicians.   B a magic show.   J street art.
3 Brianna … the restaurant.   W didn't know   Y didn't like   (C) loved
4 One evening, they went to …   (A) the theatre.   O a museum.   U the cinema.
5 They couldn't go to the museum because …   V it was closed.   H it was too far.   (N) there wasn't time.
6 Brianna wants to take grandma …   F on a tour.   (D) on a boat trip.   E shopping.

b) Now use the letters of the correct answers in a) to find Brianna's favourite place in London.

It is: **C***amden*

[1] **bacon** *der Speck*   [2] **mushroom** *der Pilz*

24 twenty-four

14 WRITING Rap Club

▶ SB, p. 24

a) Write your own rap for Rap Club — about London or another city you know.
Complete the rap with ideas from the colourful boxes or your own ideas.

(1) _____ is (2) _____

and I love living here.

There are lots of (3) _____ near, yeah it's clear.

North, south, east or west, (1) _____ is best.

We've got (3) _____, so I'm never stressed.

Sure, we have problems too:

(4) _____, it's true.

And the (5) _____ is old, not new.

But what can you do?

(1) _____ is where I grew up, this is my home!

And my (6) _____ is/are here, so I'm never alone.

And hey, you'll see, there's space for me!

And (1) _____ is the place to be.

1	name of town or city
2	amazing, cool, great
3	buses, cafés, museums, parks, people, shops, lakes, things to do
4	rubbish, traffic, noise, dirty air
5	cinema, school, skatepark, swimming pool
6	family, friends

b) Read out your rap to a partner.
If you feel brave, you can perform your rap to a group or to the class!

1 Topic 3

15 READING Green Gym[1]

a) Read the website and (circle) the three correct sentences.

▶ SB, p. 25

---

www.greengymgroup.example.com

GREEN GYM: GOOD FOR THE WORLD, GOOD FOR YOU

If you want to keep fit, you can pay lots of money for fitness classes or you can join an expensive gym. Or … you can join a Green Gym group near where you live and help your neighbourhood at the same time!

There are lots of Green Gym groups across London and the rest of the UK, so if you look at the map on our website, you'll find a group near you. We meet every week to do activities to help make our area greener. For example, we plant[2] trees, pick up rubbish and in our gardens we have free food for people who live in the neighbourhood. It's hard work, so if you help our team, you'll get as much exercise as at the gym – but it's free and more fun! And the best thing is that you'll help people too.

Green Gym is good for you too, and not just fitness. It's a great way to make new friends and we feel happier when we spend time outside each week and spend time in nature.

We have lots of different projects, so you can help in the best way for you. Everybody can join – fit or not! Email us today!

---

1 It's expensive to join Green Gym. (2 Green Gym is a project to help the area where you live.)

3 Green Gym projects take place in a building. (4 Green Gym makes you happy.)

(5 You don't need to have good fitnees to join Green Gym.)

b) Complete the sentences and give your opinion.
   Use the ideas in the box to help you complete the sentences.

I think Green Gym is …	a good project • a bad project. • great • amazing • OK • interesting • boring.	
I would/wouldn't want to join Green Gym because …	you can I want to I don't want to	get fit • help my/your neighbour-hood • make friends • meet nice people • make my/your town better.
	you don't have to	pay any money • go to a gym • do projects that are too hard • be very fit.

I think Green Gym is *(great / a good project / …*

because *you can make your town better. / …)*

I would / wouldn't like to join Green Gym because *(I want to help my neighbourhood. /*

I don't want to plant trees. / …)

---

[1] gym *das Fitnessstudio*   [2] (to) plant *pflanzen*

26 twenty-six

I can describe life in cities and in my area.

16 Viewing Josh and Jade   ▶ SB, p. 29

Read the sentences. Are they true (T) or false (F)?

1 Josh Coombes is homeless. F
2 He started a charity called *Do Something for Nothing* in 2015. T
3 Josh cuts people's hair and shows photos of the people before and after a haircut. T
4 Josh met Jade when he cut her hair. F
5 Jade helps people look after their pets. T
6 Josh and Jade feel happy because they can help people. T

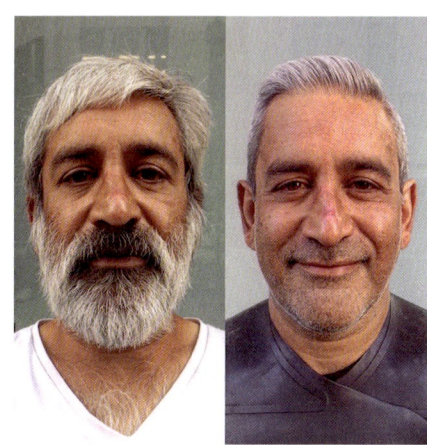

17 Viewing How to make a difference   ▶ SB, p. 29

Look at the tips from the video (1–3) and match them to the correct sentences (A–C). Then watch the video and check.

1 Involve others. — C
2 It's good to talk. — A
3 Help others, help yourself. — B

A Even if you don't have money, speaking to people and asking them about their day will make people smile.
B Helping people has made Josh happy.
C One person who saw Josh's posts is Jade, a vet who wanted to help.

18 Viewing Josh's project   ▶ SB, p. 29

Watch the first 35 seconds of the video again and write the missing words.

Josh Coombes is a hairdresser who wants to make a (1) *small* difference to people's lives. He volunteers his time and skills, giving (2) *free* haircuts to the homeless.

'I'm a hairdresser and I've been going out on the (3) *street* to cut hair for those who are homeless.'

Josh started a project called *Do Something for* (4) *Nothing*. He wants to show people that helping others is good for the community and makes you (5) *feel* good too.

twenty-seven 27

1 Wordpower

19 Food and drinks words

a) Write the words in the puzzle.

1 (across)

1 (down) Tea is a hot drink. Juice is a ... drink.

2

3 If you don't eat meat you're a ...

4 a hot drink

5

6 a cold drink

7 a chickpea dip

8

9 🍞

10 🌭

11 a kind of cheese

	1		2				
1	C	H	I	C	K	E	N	3
	O		U				V
	L	4	C	O	F	F	E	E
	D		U				G
5	T	O	M	A	T	O	E	S
			B			T	
6	L	E	M	O	N	A	D	E
		R	7		R		8
9			H		I		L
B	10	S	A	U	S	A	G	E
R			M		N		M
E			M				O
11	H	A	L	L	O	U	M	I	N
D			S				

b) Use the letters in the blue squares to write a food you often eat with a sesame sauce. _FALAFEL_

20 Verbs in Unit 1

Find the right word for each definition 1–6. Use the words in the box.

> disagree • discuss • follow • get involved in • hurry • volunteer

1 move or do something fast – _hurry_

2 work for no money – _volunteer_

3 walk or drive behind another person – _follow_

4 have a different opinion – _disagree_

5 talk about a topic – _discuss_

6 become part of something – _get involved in_

28 twenty-eight

21 Words in Unit 1

a) Write the words in the puzzle. The blue boxes will spell out a kind of building.

1 Lots of cars on the road.
2 A colour and a fruit.
3 A bike has two of them, a car has four.
4 Not too much, not too little.
5 A direction: not left, but …

1	T	R	A	F	F	I	C
2	O	R	A	N	G	E	
3	W	H	E	E	L	S	
4	E	N	O	U	G	H	
5	R	I	G	H	T		

b) Write a definition for the word in blue.

a very high building

22 Word building

Use the puzzle pieces to build the correct words. Use -ful and -less more than once.

1 When someone lives on the streets: *homeless*
2 When someone is good at everything: *successful*
3 When something is red, blue, green: *colourful*
4 When someone isn't careful: *careless*
5 When someone does things for other people: *helpful*

23 Speak English well: How do you say U?

▶ Digital help

a) How do you say "U" in the words in the box?
Write them in the correct list.
Be careful: one word is in both lists!

How do you say "U"?
Like [ʌ] as in up? Or like [juː] as in music?

bus • cucumber • menu • suddenly • tube • Tuesday • umbrella • underground • use

1 [ʌ] up, *bus, cucumber, suddenly, umbrella, underground*

2 [juː] music, *cucumber, menu, tube, Tuesday, use*

b) Now listen to the words. Were your answers in part a) right?

1 My learner log

My favourite exercise in Unit 1 was _____

because *(it was fun. / I like puzzles. / ...)* _____

I found these words and phrases in Unit 1 difficult:

_____

_____

I can remember:

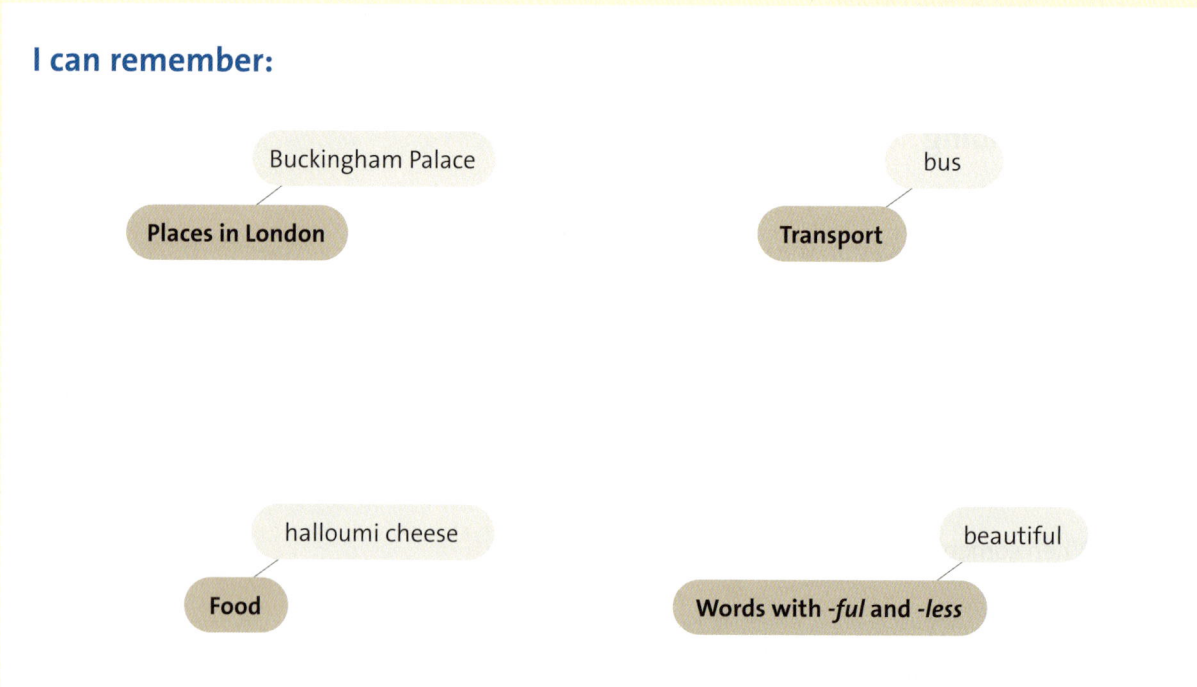

My progress[1] in English:

Use the sentence builder to write about your confidence in English.

I feel I don't feel	most confident very confident quite confident	about	reading. writing. speaking. listening.
I find	reading writing speaking listening		easy / the easiest. difficult / the most difficult. fun / the most fun.

(I feel most confident about reading. I find writing the most difficult. I feel quite confident about listening. I find speaking difficult. / ...)

[1] **progress** *der Fortschritt*

30　thirty

Early finisher 1

1 A crazy London tour

a) Write a word for each of these categories.

1. a colour (green)
2. an animal (elephant)
3. a type of transport (bike)
4. a place in London (Camden Market)
5. a different place in London (Big Ben)
6. a food (fish and chips)
7. a famous person (Adele)
8. an adjective (scary)
9. a small number (two)
10. a big number (999)

b) Turn your book upside down and use your words from a) to complete the text.

www.normaltours.example.com

Tours

(1) (green) (2) (elephant)

Welcome to our London tour! You will travel by (3) (bike) and you will see lots of interesting places, like (4) (Camden Market). We will stop for lunch at (5) (Big Ben) and you'll eat (6) (fish and chips). The tour guide will be (7) (Adele) and he/she will tell you lots of (8) (scary) stories about London! The tour will last (9) (two) hours and will cost £(10) (999).

Call now to book!

c) Write your opinion of the tour you have made.

I think my tour is (funny / weird / crazy / ...).

I would like to go on this tour because I like the tour guide / I want to see Buckingham Palace / ...

I don't want to go on this tour because (it's too long / it's boring / it's too expensive / ...)

▶ Check

1 Revision

1 London words

Write the words for the pictures, then find them in the wordsearch.

1. boat
2. bus
3. clock
4. lake
5. king
6. skyscraper
7. palace
8. roundabout
9. ticket
10. underground

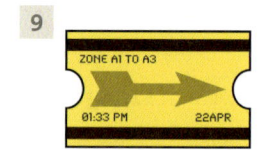

L	T	N	B	C	Q	A	Q	U	O	M
R	I	B	R	L	Q	K	I	N	G	U
G	C	U	H	O	A	A	T	D	H	G
S	K	Y	S	C	R	A	P	E	R	N
N	E	L	S	K	J	V	T	R	E	B
P	T	M	W	Y	F	K	E	G	L	O
Y	N	B	B	C	T	P	K	R	W	A
S	R	O	U	N	D	A	B	O	U	T
U	F	Y	S	A	S	L	N	U	Q	N
N	D	W	Y	O	W	A	P	N	U	T
H	B	N	T	R	O	C	U	D	Q	V
A	L	R	L	A	K	E	F	M	D	Q

2 Situations: You decide!

Write 'll or won't in the gaps.

1. It's dark. So I **won't** walk home. I**'ll** take the bus.

2. It's cold. I**'ll** make a nice cup of tea and we**'ll** sit and drink it together.

3. It's raining. So we **won't** go out. We**'ll** have a nice time at home.

4. It's late. I think I**'ll** go to bed. I **won't** finish this puzzle, but I can do that tomorrow!

5. I'm really tired. So I **won't** do my homework and I **won't** go to the gym. I**'ll** go to my bedroom and I**'ll** text a few friends.

6. My bike is broken. So I **won't** take my bike. I**'ll** hire a bike at the station.

▶ Check

3 At the Lebanese cafe

Some customers are visiting Ali's grandparents' cafe. Write the correct form of the verbs to complete the *if*-sentences.

1 If you _like_ (like) spicy food, you _'ll love_ (love) the spicy sausages they have here!

2 If I _have_ (have) enough money, I _'ll order_ (order) the chicken.

3 If they _have_ (have) it, he _'ll have_ (have) the mango milkshake.

4 If you _don't eat_ (not eat) meat, you _won't like_ (not like) the kibbeh.

5 If he _chooses_ (choose) the hummus, he _'ll order_ (order) some bread with it too.

6 If you _don't try_ (not try) the mint tea, you _'ll be_ (be) sorry because it's amazing!

4 Taking the tube

A tourist wants to travel to Camden by Underground. Write the right words from the box in the dialogue. You won't need all the words.

by • can • do • don't • goes • is • me • minutes • much • the • train • welcome

Tourist Excuse _me_, please. How _much_ is a single ticket to Camden?

Assistant £3.40 if you pay _by_ card.

Tourist And which line _is_ it for Camden, please?

Assistant You need the Northern Line.

Tourist _Do_ I need to change?

Assistant No, you _don't_.

Tourist And when is the next _train_?

Assistant There are trains every five _minutes_.

Tourist Thank you.

Assistant You're _welcome_.

▶ Check

Unit 2
Manchester: Who we are

1 My hometown¹
▶ SB, p. 45

a) Omar's hometown Manchester is very important to him. How important is your hometown to you?

Not important at all ☐ ☐ ☐ ☐ ☐ Very important

b) Explain why. Use the phrases in the box.

| I was/wasn't born here. | My friends/family are/aren't here. | There's lots/not much to do. |
| I feel … here. | I want to live … | I think it's … |

My hometown is/isn't important to me because _(I was born here. / I feel happy here. / …)_

2 Important things
▶ SB, p. 45

a) Complete the puzzle. The words are all on **pages 44 and 45** in your book.

1 When you can't use a part of your body well you have a …
2 Something which you like best.
3 Something to text people or to use the internet.
4 The mother and father of your mother and father.
5 A school for students over 11 years old.
6 Where Omar and Rosie live.
7 A ball sport with eleven people on each team.

1 D I S A B I L I T Y
2 F A V O U R I T E
3 P H O N E
4 G R A N D P A R E N T S
5 S E C O N D A R Y
6 M A N C H E S T E R
7 F O O T B A L L

b) Write the blue word from the puzzle and circle the correct meanings.

My parents _support_ me means they
1 help / don't help me a lot.
2 think that I'm right / wrong.
3 make me feel nervous / confident.

¹ **hometown** Heimatort

34 thirty-four

I can explain what's important to me.

Topic 1

3 Reading Rosie's friends
▶ SB, p. 46

Read the descriptions and circle the correct words.

1 Elena is wearing a white / (green) top and a (skirt) / dress, plus black (shoes) / glasses.
2 Jacob is wearing a red (T-shirt) / jacket, black / (blue) jeans and red (headphones) / glasses.
3 Farida is wearing a comfortable (pink) / red T-shirt and a scarf / (jacket). She's also wearing black (trousers) / shoes and long (white) / black boots.

4 Listening Manchester Fashion Week
▶ SB, p. 46

🔊 06

a) Listen to the description of a model and draw the outfit.

b) Now check on page 89. Is your drawing (almost) the same?

c) What do you like and not like about the outfit?

I think this outfit is (cool / interesting / comfortable / weird / …),

but I like / don't like the (colours / trousers / shoes /…).

thirty-five 35

5 Reading Clothes swap

▶ SB, p. 47

Read the article and then complete the sentences.

www.sustainable-fashion.example.com/news

Don't shop, swap!

How many clothes do you have in your wardrobe that you never wear? The *Stitched Up* group in Manchester can help you make space, save money and look good – and save the planet at the same time! It doesn't sell clothes at a good price, but it supports people by recycling clothes and helping people to reuse clothes.

For example, there's a monthly clothes swap. This is the perfect way to get new outfits without spending any money! You can bring clothes that you don't wear any more, and you'll get a ticket for them. Then you can swap the ticket for different clothes that cost the same price. So it's fair – you can't bring in a cheap hat and get famous brand jeans! But you can still find cool clothes. Mei Yoshida, 16, told us, "I don't have enough money to buy new clothes all the time. But last week, I brought an old shirt that's too small for me to the swap, and I found a colourful skirt that's perfect for my friend's party next weekend!"

What do you do if you have ripped your shirt or if you break a dress? Don't throw it away – our planet doesn't need more rubbish! Bring it to one of the charity's events and their experts can make it look as good as new. It's free because everyone is a volunteer. Or, if you're interested, the *Stitched Up* group has cheap weekly sewing courses[1] where you can learn how to make new clothes. And if you can't go to a weekly course, you can watch the videos on their website.

Source: https://stitchedup.coop (16.08.2023)

1 *Stitched Up* helps people to ...

a *make space in their wardrobes.*   b *save money.*

c *look good.*   d *save the planet.*

2 At a clothes swap you can *bring* old clothes and *get free* new clothes.

3 A clothes swap event is fair because you *can't bring in cheap clothes and get expensive clothes*.

4 Mei Yoshida was happy because she found *a colourful skirt that's perfect for a party*.

5 If you have ripped a shirt, for example, bring it to *Stitched Up* and *volunteers/ experts will make it look as good as new*.

6 The group's videos show you how *you can make new clothes*.

---

[1] **sewing course** *Nähkurs*

I can talk about fashion.

Topic 2

6 Reading A letter to the *Hey!* advice column
▶ SB, p. 48

a) Complete the letter with words from the box.

> brands • buy • comfortable • dear • dress • expensive • important • laugh

(1) *Dear* advice column

All my friends wear clothes from one of the cool (2) *brands*. But my parents won't

(3) *buy* me nice new clothes because they say they are too (4) *expensive*.

I don't really think new clothes are (5) *important*, but I just want to

(6) *dress* like my friends. I know that some people at school (7) *laugh*

about my old clothes, but they're (8) *comfortable*. What can I do?

Sad student ☹

b) Read the answer from *Hey!* advice column. What do you think about the advice?

Dear Sad student

It's hard when you feel different, but you don't have to change your clothes just because other people say you must dress the way they want you to.

Perhaps you can talk to your parents about this problem. Maybe you can find a weekend job and earn some money that you can spend on new clothes.

And talk to your friends and tell them how you feel. If they won't listen, then maybe instead[1] of new clothes, you need new friends?

Best wishes — The *Hey!* advice column

I think the advice is good / bad because …

☐ it's important that you dress the way you want to.

☐ it's important that you feel comfortable in your clothes.

☐ it helps to talk to people about your problems.

☐ it's not easy to follow.

---

[1] **instead** anstatt

7 LISTENING In a bus

▶ SB, p. 50

a) Two friends, Andy and Rachna, are talking in the bus on the way home from school.
Read sentences 1–6 below.
Then listen and circle the right option.

Was kannst du aus dem Dialog schließen?
Satz 1: Ende der Schulwoche – also ist der Wochentag …

1 It **is** / isn't Friday.
2 Andy is / **isn't** going to do the weekly shopping with his mum and dad.
3 Maya's wedding **is** / isn't going to be in church.
4 There **is** / isn't going to be music at the wedding party.
5 Rachna **is** / isn't going to go to a restaurant on Sunday.
6 The weather is / **isn't** going to be good on Sunday.

b) Listen again and answer the questions.

1 Who is going to come to Maya's wedding? _lots of family_
2 Where's the wedding party going to be? _Central Hotel_
3 Who's Rachna going to be with on Sunday lunchtime? _(with her) grandparents_
4 What's Andy going to do on Sunday? _(go) cycling_

8 LANGUAGE Friends and family

▶ SB, p. 50

a) The school holidays begin next week.
What are you and your school friends going to do?
In each sentence:
1 Circle the correct form of be.
2 Then write the verb in the going to-form.

1 Lisa and her brother Leon is / **are** _going to_ _stay_ (stay) with their aunt.
2 Alex **is** / are _going to_ _go_ (go) camping with a group of friends.
3 Hannah and Mara is / **are** _going to_ _see_ (see) their favourite show in Berlin.
4 Jonas is happy. He**'s** / are just _going to_ _relax_ (relax) at home.
5 **I'm** / are _going to_ _visit_ (visit) my cousins.
6 So we's / **'re** all _going to_ _have_ (have) a good break.

b) What are you and your friends not going to do? Complete the sentences with:

aren't / isn't / 'm not   going to   verb

1 Lisa and Leon **aren't going to go** (go) by car.
2 Alex **isn't going to cook** (cook) any meals.
3 Hannah and Mara **aren't going to stay** (stay) in London overnight.
4 Jonas **isn't going to travel** (travel).
5 I **'m not going to take** (take) my dog with me.
6 We **aren't going to do** (do) any school work for a few days!

9 LANGUAGE Your questions to Lisa

▶ SB, p. 50

a) Write the questions with the words in the right order.

1 going to / Are you and Leon / go by train?
   Are you and Leon going to go by train, Lisa?

2 going to / meet you / is your aunt / at the station?
   And **is your aunt going to meet you at the station?**

3 do together? / are you / going to / What
   What are you going to do together?

4 going to / come home? / When / are you both
   When are you both going to come home?

5 next week? / see you / going to / am I
   And **am I going to see you next week?**

6 like we usually do? / Are we / go to computer club / going to
   Are we going to go to computer club like we usually do?

b) And you?
Write two things that you're going to do tomorrow. And two things that you're not going to do.

I'm going to

I can make plans.

10 LANGUAGE Elena's competition ▶ SB, p. 52

a) **Rosie is talking to her friend Elena. Complete the conversation with words from the box.**

> myself • ourselves (2x) • themselves • yourself

Rosie Hey Elena, what's up? You look happy!

Elena I'm so proud of (1) *myself*, Rosie – I've just won a skateboarding competition!

Rosie That's amazing! I've always believed in you and I hope you have more confidence in (2) *yourself* now too.

Elena Well, it really wasn't easy at first, that's true. And last year, my friends and I all lost and we found it hard to believe in (3) *ourselves*. But then we thought: No, we must have confidence in (4) *ourselves* and now we're all much better skateboarders.

Rosie They sound like great friends.

Elena They are! They don't just think about (5) *themselves*. They support me and I support them. It's great.

b) **Complete the sentences about skateboarding with a reflexive pronoun.**

1 Elena really enjoys *herself* when she goes skateboarding.

2 Elena's friend Kai hurt *himself* last week when he fell over.

3 All the skateboarders were proud of *themselves*, even if they didn't win the competition last year.

4 Being a good sportsperson means you shouldn't just think about *yourself*.

5 Elena says, 'I feel good about *myself* when I know I've tried hard.'

6 Doing a sport we love can help us to have more confidence in *ourselves*.

Topic 3

11 LISTENING A confident Lioness[1]   ▶ SB, p. 53

a) Omar's friend Dev talks about Hannah Blundell.
Read the sentences and listen.
Are the sentences true (T) or false (F)?

1 Dev doesn't like Hannah Blundell. **F**
2 The women's England football team is called the Lionesses. **T**
3 Hannah has always been good at football. **F**
4 She was successful in her first team. **F**
5 Chelsea didn't want Hannah to play for them at first. **T**
6 Hannah never played for Chelsea. **F**
7 Hannah plays for Manchester United now. **T**

b) Listen again and correct the false sentences from a).

1 Dev likes Hannah Blundell.

3 Hannah hasn't always been good at football.

4 She wasn't successful in her first team.

6 Hannah played for Chelsea when she was 19.

12 WRITING How do you feel?   ▶ SB, p. 54

Complete the sentences about yourself. Use ideas from the box or your own ideas.

> maths lessons • my friends • party • show • swimming maths lesson • …

1 I often feel happy when _I'm with my friends_.

2 I feel excited when _(I'm going to see a good show.)_

3 I sometimes feel bored when _(I'm sitting in a maths lesson.)_

4 I usually feel shy when _(I go to a party.)_

5 I feel confident when _(I go swimming.)_

---

[1] **lioness** die Löwin

| Topic 1 | Topic 2 | **Topic 3** | Story | Wordpower |

13 SPEAKING Ways to be more confident
▶ SB, p. 54

a) Omar has found two adverts for helping people with their confidence. Work with a partner.
Partner B: Look at **page 90**.
Partner A: Ask your partner these questions and write the answers.

1 What's your advert for? *It's for a 'confidence club' at school.*

2 How can it help people be more confident? *They can learn to act, dance and talk in public.*

3 When can people do this? *Every Thursday at lunchtime.*

4 How can they try this activity? *They should speak to Mrs Gibson.*

b) Read the advert and answer your partner's questions.

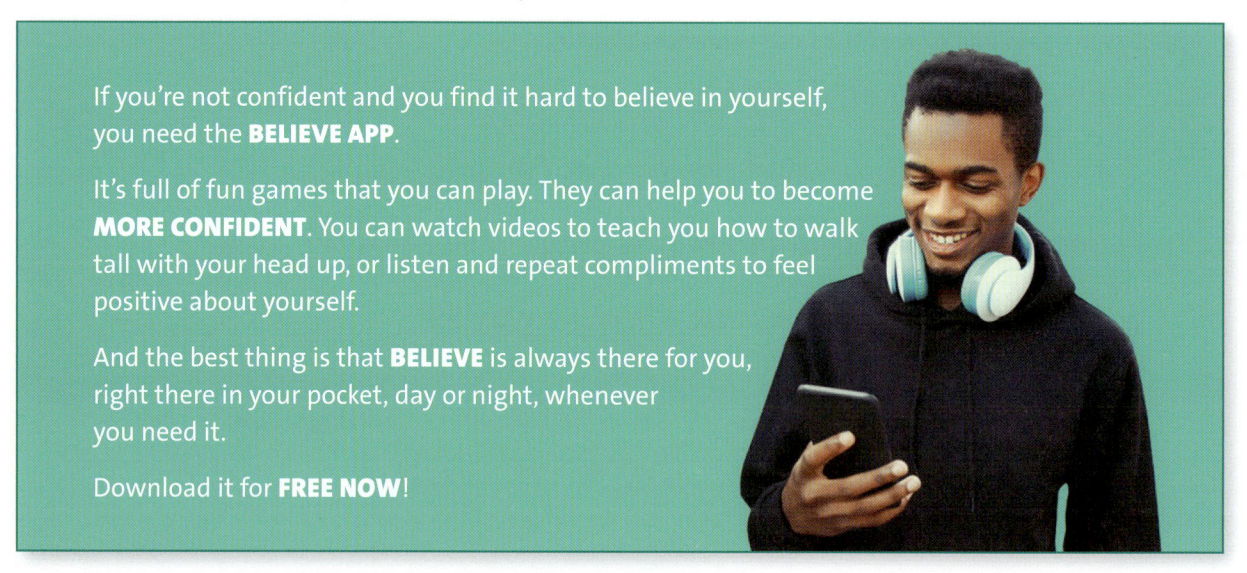

> If you're not confident and you find it hard to believe in yourself, you need the **BELIEVE APP**.
>
> It's full of fun games that you can play. They can help you to become **MORE CONFIDENT**. You can watch videos to teach you how to walk tall with your head up, or listen and repeat compliments to feel positive about yourself.
>
> And the best thing is that **BELIEVE** is always there for you, right there in your pocket, day or night, whenever you need it.
>
> Download it for **FREE NOW**!

c) Which activity do you think is best and why? Write the answer and then tell your partner.
I like *(the app best because you can use it whenever you like. / I don't like acting. / I like the 'confidence club' best because you can make friends. / I like dancing. / ...)*

14 WRITING Compliments
▶ SB, p. 55

Write one or two nice things about a friend in their workbook, and ask them to write something nice about you here. (You'll find examples on **page 55** in your student's book).
Come back to this page and read it when you need a confidence boost.

You're good at maths. / You're a kind friend. / You try hard. / ...

I can **talk about confidence.**

15 Reading Who, what, where, how, why?
▶ SB, pp. 56–57

Answer the questions about the story.

1. Which teams do Omar and Trent support?

   Omar: *Manchester City*

   Trent: *Manchester United*

2. Where does the story take place? At a *football match.*

3. Who is Ollie? Trent's *cousin.*

4. How did Omar and Trent talk during the match? They *texted.*

5. Why were some of the fans unhappy after the match? Because their team *lost the match.*

6. What did Ollie do? He called Omar and his family racist names *and pushed Omar's dad.*

16 Words in the story
▶ SB, pp. 56–57

Find the football words in the story for each definition.

1. Someone who really likes a football team: *supporter*
2. Where the football players play *(two answers)*: *stadium / pitch*
3. The footballer who stops goals: *goalkeeper*
4. When you loudly support your team: *cheer*
5. How many goals each team has got: *score*
6. When the match takes a bit longer: *additional time*

17 Writing Football and you
▶ SB, pp. 56–57

**Do you watch football or play football? Is football important to you? Why or why not?
Write at least three sentences.**

(I don't play football, but I watch football.

My favourite team is …

I sometimes go and watch live matches./ …)

I can **discuss a conflict in a story.**

18 Words to describe people and things

Complete the words with vowels (a, e, i, o, u) or y.

1. fast: q u i c k
2. not rich: p o o r
3. not old: y o u n g
4. not confident: s h y
5. not in danger: s a f e
6. well, not sick: h e a l t h y
7. not easy: d i f f i c u l t
8. important, not funny: s e r i o u s

19 Words that go together

Complete the sentences with a red word and a blue word in each sentence.

do • give • have • keep • say • take

advice • care • crush • sorry • trying • well

1. If a friend needs help, you can **give** them **advice**.
2. If you **have** a **crush** on another student it means you are in love with them.
3. Work hard for your exam and you will **do** very **well**.
4. What she did was wrong and she should **say** **sorry** to her friend.
5. They love their sister and **take** good **care** of her.
6. I don't find swimming easy, but I **keep** **trying** and I'm getting better.

20 Word families

Look at the nouns.
Then complete the adjectives in the same word family with: -al, -ing, -ful, -less.

1. centre: There's lots of traffic in centr**al** Manchester.
2. annoy: It's annoy**ing** when people only see my disability!
3. interest: I find listening to people is very interest**ing**.
4. care: Is your brother a care**ful** or a care**less** driver?
5. addition: We were very lucky and scored a goal in addition**al** time.
6. frustration: This puzzle is difficult. I find it very frustrat**ing**.

Wordpower 2

21 Wrong word!

Which word is wrong? Write the wrong word and say why it's wrong with a word from the box.

~~clothes~~ • compliment • football • person • time

1 dress   shirt   skirt   wear

Wear is wrong because it isn't a _clothes_ word.

2 confidence   yesterday   tonight   tomorrow

Confidence is wrong because it isn't a _time_ word.

3 conflict   penalty   goalkeeper   half-time

Conflict is wrong because it isn't a _football_ word.

4 amazing   beautiful   terrible   comfortable

Terrible is wrong because it isn't a _compliment_.

5 friend   problem   enemy   boyfriend

Problem is wrong because it isn't a _person_.

22 SPEAKING Speak English well: F and V

a) Listen to the words 'ferry' and 'very' and repeat.

b) Listen to the words and write if they have an 'F-sound' or a 'V-sound'.

Remember:
English **V** sounds like German **W**.

1 _F_	2 _V_	3 _V_	4 _F_	5 _V_
6 _F_	7 _F_	8 _V_	9 _F_	10 _V_

c) Listen to the words again and repeat.

d) Tic-Tac-Toe: Work with a partner.
Take turns to say a word, then colour in that box. Can you get three boxes in a row?   ▶ Digital help

ferry	safe	off
gift	five	save
love	very	give

forrty-five 45

2 My learner log

In Unit 2, I was most interested in learning about *(Manchester / football / …)*

_____

because *(I want to visit Manchester. / I'm very sporty. / …)*

I can make plans
- *(I'm going to fly to Rome next week. / …)*
- *(I'm not going to go there with my parents. / …)*
- *(When are you going to come back? / …)*

I can write sentences with
- myself: *(I don't like looking at myself in the mirror. / …)*
- herself: *(My mum taught herself to play the piano. / …)*
- themselves: *(My classmates really believe in themselves. / …)*
- (not) allowed to: *(I'm not allowed to watch scary films. / …)*

I know lots of football words
team, stadium, half-time, penalty, additional time, cheer, pitch, goalkeeper

My progress in English

Write one or two words about how you find each skill or area. You can use words from the box or your own ideas..

> Don't forget you are doing great!

- Reading: *(easy / fun / …)*
- Writing: *(difficult / important / …)*
- Listening: *(interesting / best / …)*
- Speaking: *(difficult / useful / …)*
- Mediation: *(fun / useful / …)*
- Viewing: *(easy / not useful / …)*
- Language: *(most difficult / boring / …)*

> best • boring • difficult • easy • fun • important • interesting • useful • worst

[1] **progress** *der Fortschritt*

46 forrty-six

Early finisher 2

1 Fashion designer

a) Draw your own ideas for a smart outfit for a summer party or a uniform for a football team.

b) WRITING Write a description of someone wearing the clothes you have drawn. Don't forget to use adjectives and opinions. Exercise 3 on page 35 can help you. ▶ Digital help

The person is wearing *(ripped blue jeans and a long red top.*

She is also wearing yellow sunglasses and a cool hat./ ...)

I like these clothes because they're *(comfortable, but they also look good./ ...)*

2　Revision

1 Clothes

Write the words.

1. socks
2. sweater
3. tie
4. skirt
5. dress
6. trousers

2 Tips for life skills

a) **Write the right verbs from the box. You won't need all of them.**

borrow • compare • interrupt • keep • make • rest • support • tell

1. You'll never feel well if you always _compare_ yourself with other people.
2. Try to _support_ your friends when they have a problem.
3. If you need something, don't be shy! Ask a friend if you can _borrow_ it.
4. Some people are slow. Try not to _interrupt_ them when they speak.
5. If you see a friend doing something really stupid, _tell_ him or her not to do it.
6. If something doesn't work the first or second time, _keep_ trying ☺.

b) **Swap with a partner and check your partner's sentences.**

3 Opposites

Write the opposites.

1. easy ↔ d i f f i c u l t
2. ending ↔ b e g i n n i n g
3. small ↔ b i g
4. ahead ↔ b e h i n d
5. dangerous ↔ s a f e
6. quick ↔ s l o w
7. clever ↔ s t u p i d
8. yesterday ↔ t o m o r r o w
9. old ↔ y o u n g
10. confident ↔ s h y

▶ Check

4 Late for the train

Complete the text with the words in the box.

myself • yourself • herself • himself • ourselves • themselves

Mia and Adam had a weekend in Manchester and they really enjoyed (1) _themselves_.

Mia bought (2) _herself_ a few things, and Adam did the same, so on the last morning they had a very big bag to take to the station.

And then at the station Adam fell over the bag and hurt (3) _himself_.

'I don't want to see (4) _myself_ in a mirror,' he joked.

'No time for jokes,' said Mia, 'We must be quick or we'll miss our train.'

They ran as fast as they could and they got their train just in time.

'Well, we can be proud of (5) _ourselves_!' said Mia when they sat on the train.

And she got out a packet of biscuits. 'Help (6) _yourself_,' she said to Adam.

5 Lots of clubs at school

Complete the sentences with the right form of the *going to*-future.

1. What clubs _are_ we all _going to_ join this term?
2. James _is going to_ join the table tennis club.
3. And Miriam _is going to_ join the film club.
4. What club _are_ you _going to_ join, Talib?
5. Me? I_'m going to_ join the dance club.
6. And my friend Dorothy and I _are going to_ join the swimming club.

6 Opinions

Read the dialogue. Then make your own dialogue and give your opinions about two sports. Change the words in blue.

Gary   If you ask me, football is the best sport in the world.
Cath   Football? Sorry, I really don't agree with you at all!
I would say that skiing is more fun.
Gary   Skiing? Hm, maybe you're right.
But in my opinion football is the best team sport in the world!

▶ Check

Unit 3
Scotland: Adventure

1 Places in Scotland
▶ SB, p. 73

a) Read the descriptions and write the correct places from the box on the map.

Ben Nevis • Edinburgh • Eilean Donan Castle • Inverness • Loch Ness • west coast

A This is an old castle. Does it maybe have a ghost in it?	B Grace and Rhona live here, in the capital of the Highlands.
C This is a big lake. Some people think there's a monster in it!	D This is the highest mountain in Scotland and in the UK. It's a great place for hiking.
E This is a part of Scotland where you can go kayaking.	F This is the capital of Scotland. There's a castle and lots of shops for tourists.

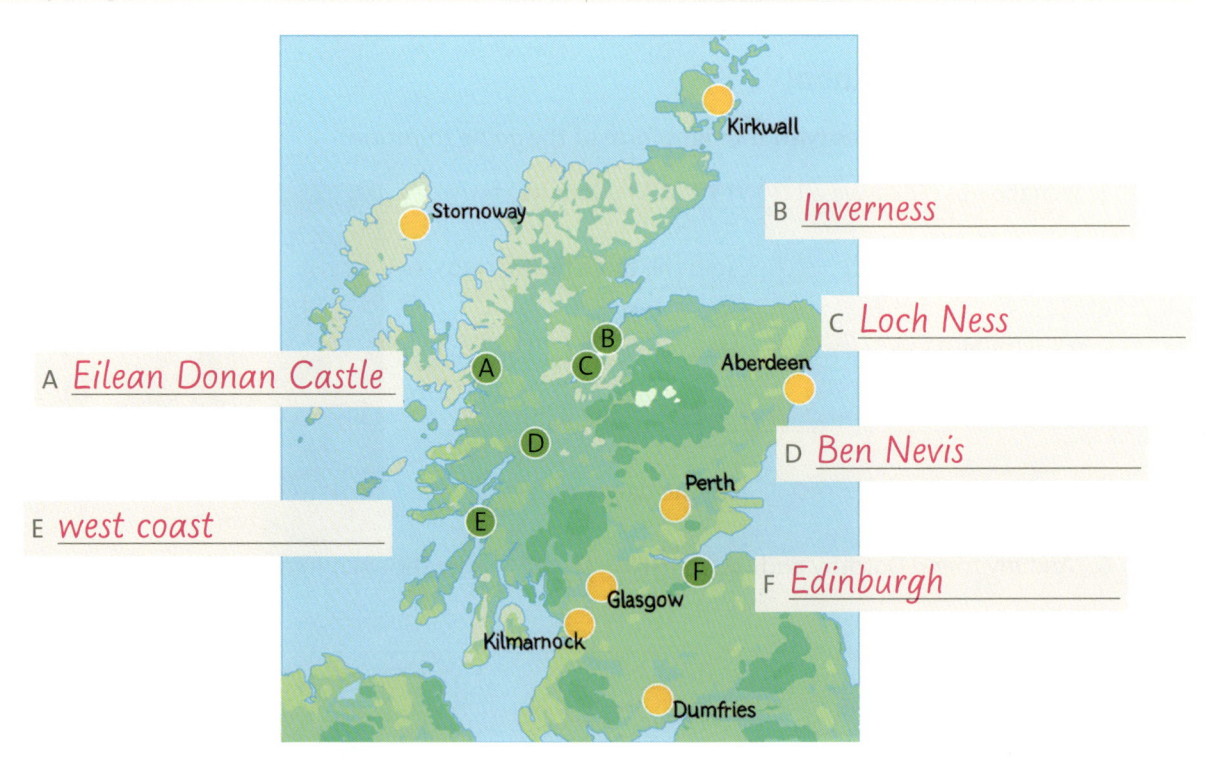

A _Eilean Donan Castle_
B _Inverness_
C _Loch Ness_
D _Ben Nevis_
E _west coast_
F _Edinburgh_

b) Look at the map and find the Scottish towns and cities.

1 This town is in the south of Scotland, near England: _Dumfries_

2 This city is on the east coast of Scotland: _Aberdeen_

3 This is the largest city in Scotland and is in the west: _Glasgow_

4 This is a town on an island in the north of Scotland: _Kirkwall_

I can **talk about Scotland.**

2 LISTENING Looking for Nessie ▶ SB, p. 75

a) Listen to a radio report¹ and interviews and tick (✓) the correct box for each person.

	doesn't believe in Nessie	isn't sure	believes in Nessie
Rory			✓
Rory's dad John		✓	
Douglas			✓
Morag			✓
The reporter	✓		

b) Listen to the report again and circle the correct words.

1 The legend of the Loch Ness Monster is new / **very old**.
2 Hundreds of people have come to Loch Ness to **look for** / make a film about the monster.
3 More people are watching the event in the cinema / **at home**.
4 Some people are next to the lake, others are in a plane / **boats**.

Make listening easier: Read the sentences before you begin listening 😊.

c) Now listen to the interviews again and complete the words.

1 A boy called Rory says Nessie maybe has _babies_ at the bottom of the lake.

2 His dad says that he likes not knowing if Nessie is _real_ or not.

3 Some people saw a monster with a long _neck_.

4 But it wasn't the real monster – it was a monster from a _film_.

Make listening easier: Guess the words before you begin listening 😊.

¹ **radio report** der Radiobericht

3 The legend of the Blue Men of the Minch

▶ SB, p. 76

a) READING Read the play and circle the four correct sentences.

① Finlay is Lorna and Jamie's grandpa.
② Finlay says they shouldn't go to the Minch Sea.
③ The Blue Men of the Minch can be dangerous for people in boats.
④ Jamie isn't nice to the Blue Man.
⑤ The Blue Man wants them to tell him a poem.
⑥ The Blue Man likes what Lorna says.

b) LANGUAGE 'Carefully' is an adverb. Highlight ten more adverbs in the play.

Scene 1

(Jamie, a young fisherman[1], and his sister Lorna are carefully packing for a fishing trip[2].)

Finlay	Where are you going fishing today, Jamie and Lorna?
Jamie	In the Minch Sea, near the island of Lewis, Grandpa.
5 Finlay	Be careful, then. That's the home of the Blue Men of the Minch.
Lorna	(excitedly) Are they real, Grandpa?
Finlay	Aye, they are. They're people with blue bodies who live in the sea, and they can sink your boat if they are angry. But they love to hear poems.

Scene 2

10 (Jamie and Lorna are at sea, but it's very windy and they are trying hard to keep the boat safe. A Blue Man comes out of the water, singing beautifully.)

Lorna	The Blue Men of the Minch! They're real!
Jamie	(politely) Please don't sink our boat, Blue Man. We are only fishing for food to eat.
Blue Man	(singing) You can both go safely home
15	If first you tell us a lovely poem.
Jamie	(quietly to Lorna) That's right – Uncle Finlay said the Blue Men love poems. We must think of a poem fast!
Lorna	(thinks for a moment then says confidently) The sea is blue, the sun is warm. Oh, Blue Men, please don't make a storm.
20	We always take good care of the sea, so please let us get home safely.
Blue Man	(singing happily) Because you show respect for our water, You can go free, young son and daughter. (The Blue Man swims quickly down into the water.)
25 Jamie	Well done, Lorna!

c) What do you think about the legend? Do you like it? Why? Or why not?

I think the legend of the Blue Men of the Minch (is interesting. / boring. / (not) true. / …)

I like it ☐ / I don't like it ☐ because (I love legends. / …)

---

[1] **fisherman** der/die Fischer(in)   [2] **fishing trip** der Angelausflug

Topic 1

4 LANGUAGE Adverbs
▶ SB, p. 77

a) Read the sentences and write the adverbs in the puzzle to find a Scottish city.

1. She was angry and spoke …
2. Is Hamid sad? He spoke so …
3. Donna is a fast runner. She runs so …!
4. It isn't safe. Or can we make a fire … ?
5. They were hungry and looked at the food …
6. Leila is always polite. She asked for something to drink so …
7. Ben is a good swimmer. He swims …

1. ANGRILY
2. SADLY
3. FAST
4. SAFELY
5. HUNGRILY
6. POLITELY
7. WELL

b) The word in blue is *Glasgow*. This is a city in *Scotland*.

5 LANGUAGE Scottish ghosts
▶ SB, p. 77

Look at the pictures. Use the adjectives in the box and turn them into adverbs to complete the sentences.

angry • careful • fast • good • happy • sad

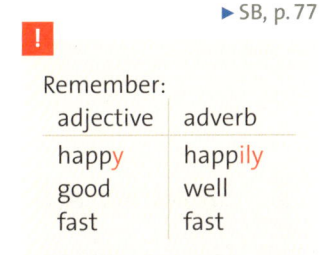

Remember:

adjective	adverb
happy	happily
good	well
fast	fast

1. The Grey Lady is singing *well*. 
2. The soldier is walking *fast*. 
3. The little boy is crying *sadly*. 
4. The girl in the white dress is laughing *happily*. 
5. The headless man is carrying his head *carefully*. 
6. Greyfriars Bobby is barking *angrily*.

I can understand stories and legends.

6 Sports

▶ Digital help ▶ SB, p. 78

Complete the Venn diagram with the sports in the box. One sport doesn't fit in the diagram.

Box: basketball • cliff jumping • cold water swimming • ~~football~~ • hiking • ice hockey • kayaking • skiing • snowboarding • surfing • underwater hockey

Venn diagram:
- Team sports: football, basketball
- Water sports: kayaking, surfing, cliff jumping
- Winter sports: snowboarding, skiing
- Team ∩ Water: underwater hockey
- Team ∩ Winter: ice hockey
- Water ∩ Winter: cold water swimming
- Outside the diagram: hiking

7 SPEAKING A timetable for an adventure sports centre

▶ SB, p. 78

a) This is a timetable from a brochure for an adventure sports centre. Some information is missing.
Partner B: Look at page 90.
Partner A: Ask your partner for the missing information and answer their questions.

How much does go-karting cost on Monday at 9 o'clock?

Ten pounds.

What can you do on Monday at 3 o'clock?

...

	9 o'clock		12 o'clock		3 o'clock	
Monday	go-karting	£10	skiing	£30	swimming	£5
Tuesday	snowboarding	£30	kayaking	£15	mountain biking	£25
Wednesday	cliff jumping	£20	mountain biking	£25	snowboarding	£30
Thursday	swimming	£5	go-karting	£10	cliff jumping	£20
Friday	kayaking	£15	swimming	£5	skiing	£30

b) Decide with your partner which three activities you would both like to do. When are they and how much will it cost in total?

I'd like to go ... because it's my favourite activity.

We can go ... at ... o'clock on ... and at ... o'clock on ... It costs ...

8 LANGUAGE A young adventurer ▶ SB, pp. 79

a) Read the article. Highlight the eight verbs in the present perfect.

Remember, verbs in the present perfect have two parts.

A young mountain adventurer

Quinn Young from Inverness **has climbed** all the Munros in Scotland. A Munro is a Scottish mountain that is over 3,000 feet or 914 metres high. Many hikers **have tried** to climb them all – but little Quinn is special: she **has done** it at the age of 10!

Quinn, who **has lived** in Scotland all her life, started climbing at the age of four with her dad, Ian, and she got to the top of Ben Nevis just before her fifth birthday.

She carries her own water, food and extra clothes, and she **hasn't needed** any help, even in bad weather, her dad explained.

Over 7,000 people **have finished** the challenge officially, climbing all 282 Munros in Scotland, but most of them were adults. Now Quinn **has joined** this list of adventurers. She and her dad **haven't tried** to climb Mount Everest yet, but we're sure Quinn can do it!

Ben Nevis

b) Now read the questions and complete the answers with verbs in the present perfect.

1 What has Quinn Young done?
   She *has* *climbed* all the Munros.

2 What is this so special?
   She *has* *done* it by the age of ten.

3 How long has Quinn Young lived in Scotland?
   She *has* *lived* in Scotland all her life.

4 Has Quinn's dad needed to help her?
   No, she *hasn't* *needed* any help.

5 How many people have climbed all 282 Munros?
   Over 7,000 people *have* *climbed* all 282 Munros.

6 Have Quinn and her dad tried to climb Mount Everest?
   No, they *haven't* *tried* to climb Mount Everest yet.

9 LANGUAGE Irregular verbs in the present perfect

▶ SB, pp. 80–81

a) Complete the questions with the past participle of a verb in the table.

Some past participles end in -en: be, break, drive, forget, ride	Some past participles look the same as the infinitive: read, put	Some past participles with other changes: do, sleep, swim

1 Have you ever **been** scared of ghosts?
2 Have you ever **broken** a leg?
3 Have you ever **driven** a car?
4 Have you ever **forgotten** to pay for something?
5 Have you ever **ridden** a horse?
6 Have you ever **read** a Harry Potter book?
7 Have you ever **put** milk in your tea?
8 Have you ever **done** your homework in the bus?
9 Have you ever **slept** in a tent?
10 Have you ever **swum** in the sea?

b) Practise questions 1–10 with a partner.

Have you ever ...?
Yes, I have.
No, I haven't.

10 LANGUAGE Your experiences

▶ SB, pp. 80–81

Write five sentences about what you have often or never done.
You can use the ideas in the box to help you.

I've	often never	played rugby. • table tennis. • ... worked in a shop. • in our garden. • ... met a famous person. • a film star. • ... been to ... • visited ... • cooked ... • seen ... • had ... • ...

1 I've *often seen films about Nessie.*
2 I *('ve never played rugby. / ...)*
3 I *('ve often been to Berlin. / ...)*
4 *(I've never cooked a meal. / ...)*
5 *(I've never had a dog. / ...)*
6 *(I've often visited my grandparents in Turkey. / ...)*

I can talk about activities and adventures.

11 Writing Problems in nature

▶ SB, p. 82

TIPS FOR PROTECTING NATURE
DON'T …
- make a fire!
- leave the gate open!
- leave rubbish!
- feed the animals!
- take flowers!
- leave the path!

Some people have not followed the tips for protecting nature. Look at the picture and say what somebody has done.

💡

Five sentences – good!
Six sentences – great!

1 Somebody has *made a fire.*
2 Somebody *has left the gate open.*
3 Somebody *has left rubbish.*
4 *Somebody has fed the animals.*
5 *Somebody has taken flowers.*
6 *Somebody has left the path.*

12 MEDIATION How to help
▶ SB, p. 83

Read the advert and summarize it in German.

> **Help protect birds in your area** 
>
> The number of different kinds of birds has gone down across Scotland and the rest of the UK and our birds need your help! Luckily, there are a lot of things we can all do to protect them.
> - Leave out food for them to eat, plus fresh water for drinking and cleaning. But don't do this if you have a cat!
> - Don't feed wild birds bread or rice as it's not healthy for them.
> - Download our app and send photos of birds you see in your area to help us with our research.

(Es gibt nicht mehr so viele Vogelarten in Schottland und Großbritannien wie früher. Man kann den Tieren helfen, indem man Futter auslegt, aber nur wenn man keine Katze hat. Brot oder Reis sind schlecht für Vögel. Und wenn man sich die App holt, dann kann man Bilder einsenden und damit der Forschung helfen.)

13 Nature in your area
▶ Digital help ▶ SB, p. 83

a) Write the correct nature word for each picture, then tick (✓) the ones that are in your area.

1. cliffs
2. mountains 
3. lake 
4. river 
5. coast 
6. horses 
7. seagulls 
8. forest 

b) SPEAKING Tell your partner about your favourite place in nature in your area, what you can see there and why you like it. You can use these ideas or your own ideas.

My favourite place in nature is	next to … • at the top of … • not far from …
When I'm there I like	looking at the stars. • the water. • the grass. • the farm animals. • …
If I'm lucky I sometimes see	some wild animals. • some horses. • …
I like it there because	it's beautiful. • quiet. • …

I can talk about nature. ✓

14 VIEWING What happens in the video
▶ SB, p. 87

Read the text and circle the correct information. Then watch the video and check.

Mon lives in Scotland / **(Norway)** and has made a vlog about a boat trip / **(road trip)**. It's her **(first)** / second time in Scotland and it's new for Mon and her friend George to drive on the right / **(left)** side of the road. In her vlog, Mon explores a lot of different **(castles)** / islands and then visits the city of Glasgow / **(Inverness)**. Mon and George swim / **(don't swim)** on the Isle of Skye because the water is **(cold)** / warm. Mon climbs down a **(valley)** / mountain to a small river, then on the last day, they listen to traditional **(music)** / poems.

15 Words in the video
▶ SB, p. 87

Write the correct words from the box.

cave • coast • Highlands • valley

1 the land next to the sea: **coast**

2 a large hole in a mountain: **cave**

3 the space between two high mountains: **valley**

4 the mountains in Scotland: **Highlands**

16 WRITING A scene from the video
▶ SB, p. 87

Choose one scene from the video. Write three sentences about it.
Extra: Write about one more scene. ☺

1 Inverness
2 Dunnottar Castle
3 Loch Ness

(1 This is Inverness. I can see a bridge across a river. I can also see a tower. I think it's a church / ...)

(2 This is Dunnottar Castle. It's an old and big castle. There are dark clouds in the sky. / ...)

(3 This is Loch Ness. Some people believe that a monster lives in the lake. Mon and George go horse riding at Loch Ness. / ...)

3 Wordpower

17 Some four-letter words

Read the definitions. Then match the coloured words on the right with the right definitions.

1 Not real (e.g. news). — *fake*
2 Tall, like a mountain. — *high*
3 Between your head and your body. — *neck*
4 Where you sleep in a campsite: in a … — *tent*
5 Scientists say we should eat … meat. — *less*
6 From the top of a mountain you have a beautiful … — *view*
7 Where's my phone? I can't find it! It's … — *gone*
8 I saw Jen and Jake and they were … very happy. — *both*

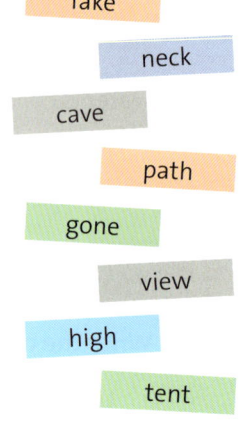

both | less | fake | neck | cave | path | gone | view | high | tent

18 Crossword

Complete the crossword puzzle.

1 Not anybody.
2 People do this when they're sad.
3 You can't stand in … water.
4 People … against unfair things.
5 A person who is in an army[1] and wears its uniform.
6 Green things that grow in nature.
7 Like a plane, used for rescues in the mountains.
8 A small way for hikers in nature.
9 Name of the high mountains in Scotland.
10 A monster.
11 An umbrella … you from the rain.
12 A way through a mountain or under a river.
13 This is how you feel when you have done something stupid.

Across/Down answers filled in:
- 5 SOLDIER
- 8 PATH
- 9 HIGHLANDS
- 11 PROTECTS
- 12 TUNNEL
- 13 EMBARRASSED
- 1 down: NOBODY
- 2 down: CRY
- 3 down: DEEP
- 4 down: PROTEST
- 6 down: PLANTS
- 7 down: HELICOPTER
- 10 down: CREATURE (shown as C O T O P E T E... letters visible: C, O, T, O, P, T, E)

[1] **army** *die Armee*

19 An adventure in the Scottish mountains

Write the correct verbs in the text.

> blamed • carried • ~~decided~~ • got lost • left • made • packed • rescued • shouted • slept

One day during our holiday in Scotland we _decided_ to go hiking. We _packed_ food for a picnic lunch and we both _carried_ big rucksacks. We had beautiful views of the mountains, but somewhere we _made_ a mistake and we _left_ the path. And then we _got lost_ in a valley and couldn't find our way back. My boyfriend was scared and _blamed_ me for not reading the map correctly. Then we both _shouted_ loudly. Luckily a hiker heard us and _rescued_ us from the horrible valley. That night we _slept_ well!

20 Word families

Complete the word families in the table.

verb	noun	adjective
protest	protester	✗
protect	protector	protective
instruct	_instructor_	instructive
✗	_nature_	natural
choose	_choice_	chosen
live	_life_	live (e.g. live music)
excite	excitement	_excited_ and _exciting_

21 LISTENING Speak English well: Word stress

Listen to the words and underline the stressed[1] syllable[2].

| 1 <u>E</u>dinburgh | 2 ad<u>ven</u>ture | 3 re<u>lax</u> | 4 <u>val</u>ley |
| 5 un<u>for</u>tunately | 6 subma<u>rine</u> | 7 <u>sol</u>dier | 8 <u>tun</u>nel |

[1] **stressed** betont [2] **syllable** die Silbe

3 My learner log

Something new I learned about Scotland in Unit 3 is that: *(Some people think there's a monster in Loch Ness. / They use different words. / ...)*

How confidently I can do these things

Write an adverb or a phrase for each of the *I can* statements. You can use ideas from the table or your own ideas.

confidently	not confidently
quite well very well	not very well yet
without help	with help

Do you make mistakes? No worries! Mistakes mean that you have learned something new. ☺

1. I can talk about Scotland *(confidently. / ...)*
2. I can understand stories and legends *(very well. / ...)*
3. I can talk about adventures and interests *(without help. / ...)*
4. I can talk about nature *(not confidently. / ...)*
5. I can discuss good and bad choices in a story *(quite well. / ...)*
6. I can structure ideas for a story *(with help. / ...)*
7. I can write a short adventure story *(very confidently. / ...)*

My next steps

Think about what you find difficult and write how you are going to improve.
You can use ideas from the box or your own ideas.

	ask	my teacher / other students / ...	for help / feedback / ...
	practise	speaking / ... English	with other students / my parents / ...
I'm going to	read	more in English.	
	listen	to English	in movies / games / ...
	use	a dictionary / an app	to learn more words.
	find	discussion phrases	in my student's book.

I am going to *(ask my teacher for help. / I am going to find discussion phrases in my student's book. / ...)*

Early finisher 3

1 Reading A ghost hunter

Read the ghost hunter's blog and answer the questions.

> Hi, I'm Sarah and my hobby is looking for ghosts! About once a month, I go to a haunted house[1] with my friends – for example, Eilean Donan Castle or one of the underground tunnels in Edinburgh – and we stay awake all night, listening for ghosts!
>
> In five years of looking for ghosts, I've never seen a ghost walking around, but I'm sure I've heard them. Once, we were in a very old house and we heard footsteps[2] in the hall – but there was nobody else in the house! Another time, I saw a glass moving on a table in a room with nobody in it! I've also taken photos in dark, empty rooms and then found white lights in the photos. My friends said these lights were ghosts.
>
> It's not a hobby for everyone, but I don't think people need to be scared when they look for ghosts because I believe most ghosts are friendly and just want to say hello.

1 What does Sarah do for her hobby?
   She stays awake all night and looks for ghosts.

2 How many ghosts has Sarah seen?
   None. / Zero. / No ghosts.

3 Does Sarah believe in ghosts? Why (not)?
   Yes, because she says she has heard them and seen photos of them.

4 Is Sarah scared during ghost hunts? Why (not)?
   No, because she believes most ghosts are friendly.

5 Would you like to go ghost hunting? Why (not)?
   (Yes / No, because it sounds exciting. / I don't believe in ghosts. / …)

▶ Check

2 Words Scotland in words

Find more words in the wordsearch. ↔ ↕
**Six more words? OK.
Ten more words? Great!**

C	L	I	F	F	S	D	L	P	K	Q	R	U	V	W
A	X	H	I	K	E	T	I	C	A	V	E	S	A	N
S	B	M	O	N	S	T	E	R	W	X	L	E	L	E
T	V	U	Y	D	F	L	A	K	E	S	G	L	L	S
L	K	N	A	T	U	R	E	H	J	K	P	E	E	S
E	M	R	Q	O	U	T	D	O	O	R	Y	I	Y	I
S	Z	O	M	O	U	N	T	A	I	N	S	E	X	E

▶ Check

---
[1] **haunted house** *das Geister-, Gespensterhaus*   [2] **footstep** *der Schritt*

3 Revision

1 Words that go together

Find words in the box that go with words 1–10.

> a bag • a bike • a car • a cat from a tree • a high cliff •
> an English word • embarrassed • in a tent • hiking • nature

1 carry *a bag*
2 go *hiking*
3 climb *a high cliff*
4 drive *a car*
5 feel *embarrassed*

6 forget *an English word*
7 protect *nature*
8 rescue *a cat from a tree*
9 ride *a bike*
10 sleep *in a tent*

2 Nature

Write the words.

1 *cave*
2 *valley*
3 *flower*
4 *gate*
5 *tent*
6 *cliff*
7 *path*
8 *sheep*
9 *helicopter*

▶ Check

64 sixty-four

3 Two months in Scotland

a) Akilah, from Berlin, spent two months in a family in Scotland. Read what she wrote about her stay. Complete each sentences with the adverb form of the adjective in blue.

1 I found that people were usually very quiet and they sit very _quietly_ in trains.

2 I found that the drivers in Edinburgh were careful and all cars usually drove _carefully_.

3 The food was good and I ate _well_.

4 5 I saw some weird sports. In one of them people ran very _weirdly_ because they carried trees!

5 I heard lots of fast speakers and it wasn't easy to understand them when they spoke so _fast_!

b) What's right? Circle the adjective or adverb.

1 My neighbour was sometimes a bit (loud)/ loudly because she played the bagpipes very loud /(loudly).

2 I went to a concert and heard a young singer sing very beautiful /(beautifully). I think Scottish folk music is very (beautiful)/ beautifully.

3 I was (happy)/ happily in Scotland and my time there passed very happy /(happily).

4 A Scottish tour guide

Read the text and circle the correct words.

Craig is from Scotland and he has always live /(lived) (1) in Edinburgh. So, of course he knows the city very well.

Craig has (had)/ have (2) a number of different jobs, but he is now a tour guide and he loves it. He has always (been)/ was (3) interested in history and he loves meeting new people. As a tour guide, he has meet /(met) (4) people from more than twenty countries. He takes tourists around the city and tells them stories about some of the scariest buildings.

'I haven't saw /(seen) (5) a ghost myself, but I believe in ghosts,' he says. 'My favourite place to visit is Greyfriar's Kirkyard, where many people say they have (seen)/ saw (6) the ghost of a dog called Bobby. Lots of people have (told)/ tell (7) me that they have hear /(heard) (8) the sound of a dog near the church.'

▶ Check

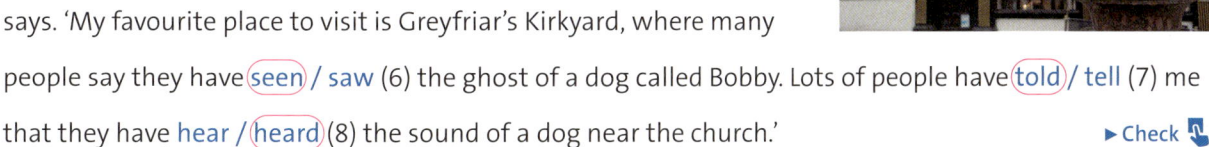

Unit 4
Wales: Digital life

1 Words, words, words
▶ SB, p. 103

a) Look at the pictures A-D on page 102 in your book. In which picture(s) can you see …

1 the sea? A, D   2 cliffs? D   3 a forest? A, B   4 a beach? A

5 a rugby team? C   6 people? A, C   7 animals? A, D   8 wind turbines? B

b) Label the animals. All the animal words are on pages 102–103 in your book.

This is a *sheep*.   This is a *donkey*.   This is a *lion*.   This is a *dragon*.

c) Write the words and the right letter A–D from the map.

1 I'm from England. I'm *English*. A

2 I'm from Wales. I'm *Welsh*. D

3 I'm from Scotland. I'm *Scottish*. B

4 I'm from Ireland. I'm *Irish*. C

d) Highlight the stressed syllable[1] in these words.

	1 national	2 million	3 digital	4 social media	5 official
in English	**na** – tion – al	**mil** – lion	**di** – gi – tal	so – cial me – dia	of – **fi** – cial
in German	na – tio – **nal**	**Mil** – lion	**di** – gi – tal	so – **zia**le **Me** – dien	of – fi – **ziell**

e) LISTENING Listen to the words from part d). Were your answers correct?
15

[1] **stressed syllable** *betonte Silbe*

sixty-six   I can understand information about Wales.

Topic 1

2 MEDIATION Gwen's video
▶ SB, p. 104

One of the students in the German exchange class has asked you to help them understand Gwen's video about Cardiff. Look at the screenshots and subtitles[1] and sum up in German.

1 	Cardiff is the capital city of Wales. It's a long way from Llandudno, but I sometimes visit it with my family.	*(Cardiff ist die Hauptstadt von Wales. Sie ist weit weg von Llandudno, aber manchmal besucht Gwen die Stadt mit ihrer Familie.)*
2 	Cardiff Castle is in the middle of the city. You can go inside and there's lots to see. I love climbing up the tower!	*(Das Schloss von Cardiff ist im Stadtzentrum. Im Schloss gibt es viel zu entdecken und einen Turm, auf den man steigen kann.)*
3 	Cardiff has a busy city centre. You'll find street musicians and food and drink from all over the world!	*(Im Stadtzentrum ist viel los: Straßenmusik sowie Essen und Trinken aus aller Welt.)*
4 	I love the beach at Cardiff Bay, with beautiful, clean sand – even if the water is usually very cold!	*(Der Sandstrand ist schön und sauber, auch wenn das Wasser meistens sehr kalt ist.)*
5 	If you like shopping, Cardiff is perfect because there are lots of shopping centres, shops and a big market.	*(Cardiff hat viele Einkaufszentren, Geschäfte und einen großen Markt.)*

3 LANGUAGE Is it yours?
▶ SB, p. 104

Replace the blue phrases in the text with a possessive pronoun: *hers, his, mine, theirs, yours*.

Owen found some sweets in the classroom. He asked Dylan, 'Are they (1) *yours* (your sweets)?'

But Dylan said no. Samara said they were (2) *hers* (her sweets), but Promit also said they were

(3) *his* (his sweets). In the end, Mr Price said sweets weren't allowed, so everyone said they

weren't (4) *theirs* (their sweets)! But really, they were (5) *mine* (my sweets) …

---

[1] **subtitles** *die Untertitel*

4 Reading A bilingual¹ school

▶ SB, p. 104

My school / Fy ysgol

Hi, I'm Gareth. I have read lots of blogs by people in other schools, so here's mine (1).

In most schools in Wales, Welsh is a school subject, but most of the lessons are in English. But our school is different. Ours (2) is bilingual. That means that we have some lessons (like maths) in English but others (like chemistry and biology) in Welsh.

I think my lessons are probably the same as yours (3). Some are interesting, some aren't! My favourite subject is probably geography, but my sister says hers (4) is music.

My grandparents are really happy about my school experience because theirs (5) was so different. There were no Welsh lessons when they were at school, because people didn't think it was useful to learn Welsh. And because of this, my parents can't really speak it. Sometimes that's a problem because they can't help me with my homework. However, it also means I have a secret language with my friends!

I'm so happy that more and more people speak Welsh now. I think it's a beautiful language and it's boring if everyone just speaks English all the time!

a) Read the blog post about life at a school in Wales and tick (✓) the right box.

Gareth's blog post is about …
1. school and sport. ☐
2. school and Gareth's sister. ☐
3. school and the Welsh language. ✓
4. school and homework. ☐

b) Read the blog post again and tick (✓) the **four correct** statements.

1. All of Gareth's lessons are in Welsh. ☐
2. Gareth learns biology in Welsh. ✓
3. Gareth's grandparents didn't learn Welsh at school. ✓
4. Gareth's parents help him with his homework. ☐
5. Gareth's parents can't understand when he speaks to his friends in Welsh. ✓
6. Welsh is more popular now than in the past. ✓
7. Gareth thinks everyone should only speak English. ☐

c) What do the five possessive pronouns in the blog post mean?

1. mine – *my blog*
2. ours – *our school*
3. yours – *your lessons*
4. hers – *her favourite subject*
5. theirs – *their school experience*

¹ bilingual zweisprachig

I can **talk about Wales.**

5 LISTENING A digital detox¹   ▶ SB, p. 107

a) Listen to Mia's podcast. Tick (✓) the correct answer.

1 Mia is excited because she's going to …
   - [✓] do something new.
   - [ ] meet a special person.

2 Mia thinks the time she spends looking at screens is …
   - [ ] OK.
   - [✓] too much.

b) Listen again and circle the correct answers.

1 Mia's project takes/took place …
   A last week.   B this week.   **(C)** next week.

2 A digital detox means …
   A only using green technology.   **(B)** not using any devices².   C cleaning your devices.

3 Mia's mum …
   (A) uses her phone a lot too.   B doesn't have a phone.   C goes out a lot.

4 At weekends, Mia uses her devices for …
   (A) more than 6 ½ hours.   B 6 ½ hours.   C half an hour.

5 Mia's family …
   A doesn't support her.   **(B)** is also going to join in the digital detox.   C doesn't have internet.

6 Maybe Mia will …
   A listen to CDs.   **(B)** read more.   C take her little sister to the park.

c) Answer the questions in 1–2 sentences.

1 Do you think a digital detox is a good idea? Why or why not?

   (Yes, because I use my phone too much. / No, because devices are very useful. / …)

2 How much screen time do you normally have each day? What do you think about this?

   I normally have (… hours of screen time a day. / …)

   I think this is (fine. / too much because it's not healthy. / …)

3 What is hard about a digital detox? Give examples.

   A digital detox is hard because you can't *text friends,* (use social media, know what is happening, get information / …)

---

¹ **digital detox** *die digitale Entgiftung, das digitale Fasten*   ² **device** *das Gerät*

4 Topic 2

6 LANGUAGE A holiday in Wales
▶ SB, p. 107

Circle the verb in the right tense and <u>underline</u> the phrase that helps you to decide which tense you need.

<u>Last week</u> we (1) have / **had** a week's holiday and we (2) go / **went** to Wales. <u>Normally</u> I (3) **text** / texted my friends every day, but I (4) don't text / **didn't text** so often <u>while I was</u> in Wales. <u>On the first day of our holiday</u> I (5) find / **found** a new online game and I really like it. I (6) play / **played** it a lot <u>while I was in Wales during the holiday</u>. I <u>always</u> (7) **try** / tried to find something nice for my grandma when I'm away. <u>On the last day</u> I (8) buy / **bought** her a little painting of the Welsh village where we (9) stay / **stayed** during our holiday.

7 READING Priya's phone call
▶ SB, p. 108

a) Priya's grandmother has called her to ask for help. Put the phone conversation in order.

6   Oh great, thank you!

2   I'm OK, thank you, Priya – but I need your help! It's this new phone. I can't *(crrr)*

4   I said I've got a new phone and I don't know how to connect it to the Wi-Fi at home.

7   You're welcome. See you tomorrow, Grandma!

1   Hi Grandma, nice to hear from you. How are things?

3   Huh? Sorry, I can't hear you, Grandma. Can you say that again, please?

5   No problem, I can come over after school tomorrow and show you.

b) LISTENING Listen and check.

c) Write the conversation in the correct order in your exercise book and answer the questions.

1   What does Priya's grandmother need help with?

She wants to connect her new phone to the Wi-Fi.

2   When will Priya help her?

Priya will help her tomorrow after school.

8 Instructions

▶ SB, p. 108

Write the instructions.
Use the words in the box and the pictures to help you.

> charge • download • swipe • switch on • switch off • tap

1. *Switch on* the phone.
2. *Swipe* to the right. 
3. *Tap* the app. 
4. *Charge* the phone. 
5. *Download* the app. 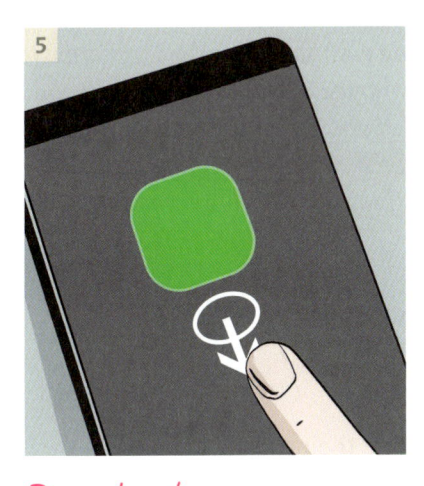
6. *Switch off* the phone. 

9 WRITING Technology and you

▶ SB, p. 109

1. Are you confident or not so confident with new technology?
   (I'm very / not so confident with new technology. / …)

2. Give examples of how you use technology.
   (I use my phone and laptop all the time. I'm learning to code at the moment. / …)

3. Write about a time you asked for or offered help with technology.
   (Last week, I helped my dad set up his new laptop. / …)

I can give simple instructions.

4 Topic 3

10 Reading Good and bad ▶ SB, p. 110

a) Read the three comments in the school magazine about social media.

www.Llandudno-school.example.com/magazine

Kali: I used to be addicted to¹ social media – I couldn't even eat a sandwich without posting a photo of it online! At first, it felt great getting so many likes and comments, but it began to take over my life. And then I found that if I uploaded a video that wasn't so popular, I felt really bad about it. In the end, I closed all my social media accounts and now I feel a lot happier.

Aled: Sure, like most people, I use a few different social media apps and I think it's a great way to make friends and stay in contact with people. It's not true that social media stops you from seeing people in real life – in fact, I send messages online to help me organise going out with friends! Plus I have family in other countries, so it's nice to share photos and videos with them. Yes, I use social media every day, but I don't think it's a problem.

JJ: I'm fine with social media. I subscribe to a few video channels and I watch them maybe three times a week. I don't upload my own videos because I'm worried about staying private online, but I like following influencers because you can learn a lot. You have to be careful and you can't just believe everything you see, but I think there's more good than bad online.

b) Decide if each question is about Kali, Aled or JJ.

1. Who uses social media the most? *Aled*
2. Who is worried about putting their private life online? *JJ*
3. Who thinks people say untrue things about social media? *Aled*
4. Who used social media a lot more in the past? *Kali*
5. Who talks about how social media can give you bad feelings? *Kali*
6. Who likes watching videos online? *JJ*

c) **Highlight** the arguments for social media in the comments.

d) Now underline the arguments against social media.

e) What do you think about social media? Give reasons for your opinion with arguments from c) and d).

I think that (social media is helpful for organizing meeting friends. / I think that social media is a problem because it can make you feel bad. / …)

¹ **addicted to** süchtig nach

11 Social media phrases

▶ SB, p. 110

Complete the verbs and finish the social media phrases with the help of both boxes.

| delete • open • pair • post • subscribe • switch | an account • an app • photos • on the sound • to a channel • a phone with a smartwatch |

1. **Delete** an account.
2. **Switch** on the sound.
3. **Post** photos.
4. **Open** an app.
5. **Subscribe** to a channel.
6. **Pair** a phone with a smartwatch.

12 LISTENING Fact or opinion?

🔊 18 ▶ SB, p. 112

a) Read texts A, B and C. Then listen to the voice note from Barri to his little sister, Kaya. Which box best describes what you hear? Tick (✓) the right box.

A
Barri is really angry because his little sister, Kaya, has done something stupid and now Barri has to come home early from his friend's house. ☐

B
Barri has read something that Kaya has written online. Barri doesn't agree with Kaya's opinion and he wants Kaya to change what she has written. ☐

C
Barri sees that Kaya doesn't understand some of the dangers of posting opinions online and of believing things that other people have written. ✓

b) Now listen again and tick (✓) the correct answer.

1. Barri is leaving a voice note because …
   - ☐ he'll be home early.
   - ☐ he can't find a website.
   - ✓ his sister shared something online.

2. He talks about a post that …
   - ☐ has lots of facts in it.
   - ✓ only has opinions in it.
   - ☐ will make his sister laugh.

3. The post was about …
   - ✓ school.
   - ☐ statistics about schools.
   - ☐ where to find information about social media.

4. Barri thinks …
   - ☐ there were too many statistics in the post.
   - ☐ the things in the post were true.
   - ✓ people should be careful about what they share.

5. Barri wants his sister to …
   - ☐ write a better post.
   - ✓ delete the post.
   - ☐ be more emotional.

13 LANGUAGE Who or what are they?

a) In which sentences can you also use who? Write who where it is possible.

1. Dafydd is a man <u>who</u> / that is eighty-six years old.
2. Ceri is a woman <u>who</u> / that can code games and websites.
3. Bethan is a robot ____ / that answers questions and plays music.
4. Elen is a robot ____ / that looks like a dog.
5. Catrin is a girl <u>who</u> / that loves reading.
6. Rhys is a boy <u>who</u> / that wears glasses.
7. Ffion is a robot ____ / that is very clever.
8. Bryn is a robot ____ / that repairs things.

b) Match the names from a) with the correct people and robots.

1. Rhys
2. Dafydd
3. Bryn
4. Catrin
5. Ffion
6. Bethan
7. Elen
8. Ceri

14 SPEAKING Explaining words

a) Partner B: Look at page 91.
Partner A: Explain the five words to your partner in sentences with who or that.
Use who if possible. Don't say the word because your partner has to guess your word! ☺

1 choir   2 biography   3 Welsh people   4 teenager   5 instruction

It's They're	a young person a book or film a sentence people a group of people	that who	is between ... and ... years old. tells you about a ... tells you what you should ... come from ... sing ...

b) Now your partner will explain five words. Write your partner's five words.

1 medicine   2 Wales   3 adults   4 cyberbully   5 dragon

I can talk about the good and bad sides of social media.

15 Reading Tell the story.

▶ SB, pp. 114–115

Read the story on pages 114–115. Then put sentences in the right order.

7	Owen posted a photo of Dylan which did not look good at all.
10	When Saskia said she liked Owen's photo of Dylan, Dylan felt better again.
2	Dylan posted a picture of a sports car and said it was their new family car.
6	Saskia was confused when she met Dylan because he looked different in his photos.
8	The photo that Owen posted got lots of mean comments.
4	Dylan wanted Owen to take lots of photos of him to post for his followers.
3	Owen and Dylan went to the beach together.
5	Dylan digitally changed a photo of himself and then posted it.
9	Owen deleted his post and felt sorry for Dylan.
1	Dylan talked online with his German exchange partner Saskia.

16 Reading Who's thinking that?

▶ SB, pp. 114–115

Decide whether Dylan, Owen or Saskia thinks each sentence.

1 'I don't understand why Dylan wrote that – it's not true!' *Owen*

2 'Wow, I'm becoming really popular online!' *Dylan*

3 'I hope Saskia thinks I look good in this photo.' *Dylan*

4 'This is strange. He's not what I expected.' *Saskia*

5 'Ha, if people laugh at him, they'll know he lied before!' *Owen*

17 Good and bad choices

▶ SB, pp. 114–115

What good and bad choices did Dylan and Owen make in the story?
Complete the notes in the table.

	good choices	bad choices
Dylan	– helped Owen with *social media.*	– put *things that weren't true* on social media.
	– stopped worrying about *how he looked online.*	– only cared about *how he looked.*
Owen	– said *sorry.*	– posted *a mean photo of Dylan* without asking.

I can talk about truth and lies on social media. ✓

4 Wordpower

18 When the line is bad …

What do you say when you can't understand somebody on the phone? Complete the words.

1 I'm sorry, I **can't** hear you.
2 Can you **hear** me now?
3 Can you say that **again**, please?
4 I'm sorry, I didn't understand **what** you said.
5 What **did** you say?
6 Ah! That's **better**. I can you hear you now.

19 Verbs in the simple past

a) Write the simple past forms of the verbs in the crossword.

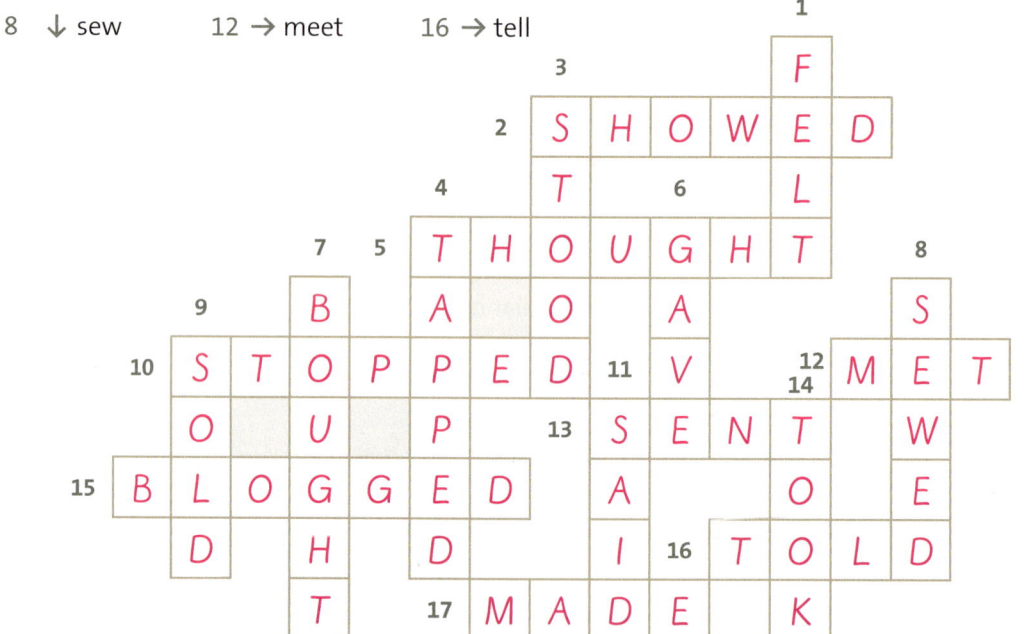

1 ↓ feel   5 → think   9 ↓ sell   13 → send   17 → make
2 → show   6 ↓ give   10 → stop   14 ↓ take
3 ↓ stand   7 ↓ buy   11 ↓ say   15 → blog
4 ↓ tap   8 ↓ sew   12 → meet   16 → tell

Crossword answers:
- 1 ↓ FELT
- 2 → SHOWED
- 3 ↓ STOOD
- 4 ↓ TAPPED
- 5 → THOUGHT
- 6 ↓ GAVE
- 7 ↓ BOUGHT
- 8 ↓ SEWED
- 9 ↓ SOLD
- 10 → STOPPED
- 11 ↓ SAID
- 12 → MET
- 13 → SENT
- 14 ↓ TOOK
- 15 → BLOGGED
- 16 → TOLD
- 17 → MADE

b) Now complete the sentences with the verbs in the simple past.

1 Gareth **blogged** (blog) about his school and **told** (tell) his friends what he **thought** (think) about it.

2 I **stopped** (stop) at the station and **bought** (buy) a book.

3 Guy **made** (make) a cake and **took** (take) it to school. Everyone **said** (say) it was good.

4 I **sewed** (sew) a dress. I **sent** (send) it to Jo and **gave** (give) it to her for her birthday.

Wordpower 4

20 Verbs in Unit 4

Write the verbs in the box in the right sentences.

> hit • lied • ordered • recognized • replied • sat • skimmed

1 We *sat* down in the restaurant and *ordered* something to eat.
2 The ball *hit* the window and the glass broke.
3 The truth was too awful, so we all *lied*.
4 When I asked a question nobody *replied*.
5 He *skimmed* the letter to find out what it was about.
6 I *recognized* you from your photo.

21 Because or because of?

(Circle) the correct word(s).

We were happy (because)/because of we were in Wales. On the first day we couldn't go swimming because/(because of) the bad weather. The next day we went to the sea (because)/because of I love swimming. We came back on Monday (because)/because of my sister had an exam the next day. But we arrived home late because/(because of) the traffic.

22 SPEAKING Speak English well: the letter W

a) Listen and repeat the words. Which word doesn't have a W sound? Cross it out (~~cross out~~).

1 Wales   2 Wi-Fi   3 walk   4 watch
5 which   6 ~~who~~   7 when   8 worry

b) Look at yourself in a mirror when you say the words.
Tick (✓) the correct mouth shape for a W sound in English.

c) Listen and repeat the tongue twister. Focus on the W sounds.

> Why would we walk to Wales when we can watch wonderful waterfalls in the wild?

4 My learner log

In Unit 4, I was most interested in learning about *(social media / Wales / …)*

because *(I want to be an influencer. / I've never visited Wales. / …)*

My progress[1]

Write an adjective to describe how you found each of the *I can* statements.
You can use ideas from the box or your own ideas.

boring • difficult • easy • (not) important • interesting • scary • useful

💡 Remember: everything is difficult before it becomes easy!

1. I can understand information about Wales: I found this *(easy. / …)*
2. I can talk about Wales: I found this *(a bit boring. / …)*
3. I can give simple instructions: I found this *(difficult. / …)*
4. I can talk about the good and bad sides of social media: I found this *(interesting. / …)*
5. I can talk about truth and lies on social media: I found this *(important. / …)*
6. I can make a talk flow: I found this *(quite difficult. / …)*
7. I can give a short talk: I found this *(scary. / …)*

Thinking about how I improved

Look back at your learner log for Unit 3 on page 62. Which things did you do to improve?

I wrote …	I practised … with …
I read more …	I listened to …
I asked … for help.	I tried learning / reading / …

(I practised the new vocabulary with my brother. /

I tried reading English online. /

I listened to English songs. /

I asked my class mates for help. / …)

[1] **progress** *der Fortschritt*

Early finisher 4

1 WRITING Before and after
▶ Digital help

a) Photo A is a photo of an influencer. In photo B she had digitally changed what she really looks like. Write what's different in photo B. Think about hair, make-up, position, lighting and filters.

In photo B the influencer's hair is different because it isn't straight.
In photo B she is wearing more make-up. She is standing/sitting in a different position. I think she has used a filter because her skin looks too perfect.)

b) Do you like the second picture or not? Say why.

I like the second picture because (she looks good. / …)
I don't like the second picture because (it doesn't look like her anymore and it's not real. / …)

▶ Check

2 Break the code

Dylan has used an app to put some words into code. Break the code and write the words!

#	%	*	]	◇	⌐	≠	{	=	>	≤	≈	}
a	b	c	d	e	f	g	h	i	j	k	l	m
△	<	≥	@	⌐	§	£	□	±	+	‼	♪	[
n	o	p	q	r	s	t	u	v	w	x	y	z

1 ≥#=⌐   *pair*
2 §+=≥◇   *swipe*
3]◇≈◇£◇   *delete*
4 *{#⌐≠◇   *charge*
5 §+=£*{ <△   *switch on*
6 £#≥   *tap*

▶ Check

4 Revision

1 Technology verbs

Write the correct words. You'll need all the letters in the box.

1. Look, 9%! It's an old phone, I need to **charge** it every day!
2. I **subscribe** to five different film channels.
3. Sorry, I don't know what she wrote because I always **delete** my messages.
4. If my phone messages are too long, I don't really read them. I just **skim** them.
5. Please **reply** as soon as you can when you get my text.
6. To open an app, **tap** the icon.
7. When you leave the office, **swipe** a card at the door.
8. And at the end of the day, please **switch** off the lights.

a • a • b • c • c •
e • e • e • e • e •
g • h • i • i •
l • m • p • p •
r • r • t • t • y

2 More technology words

Write the correct words to label the pictures of the devices.

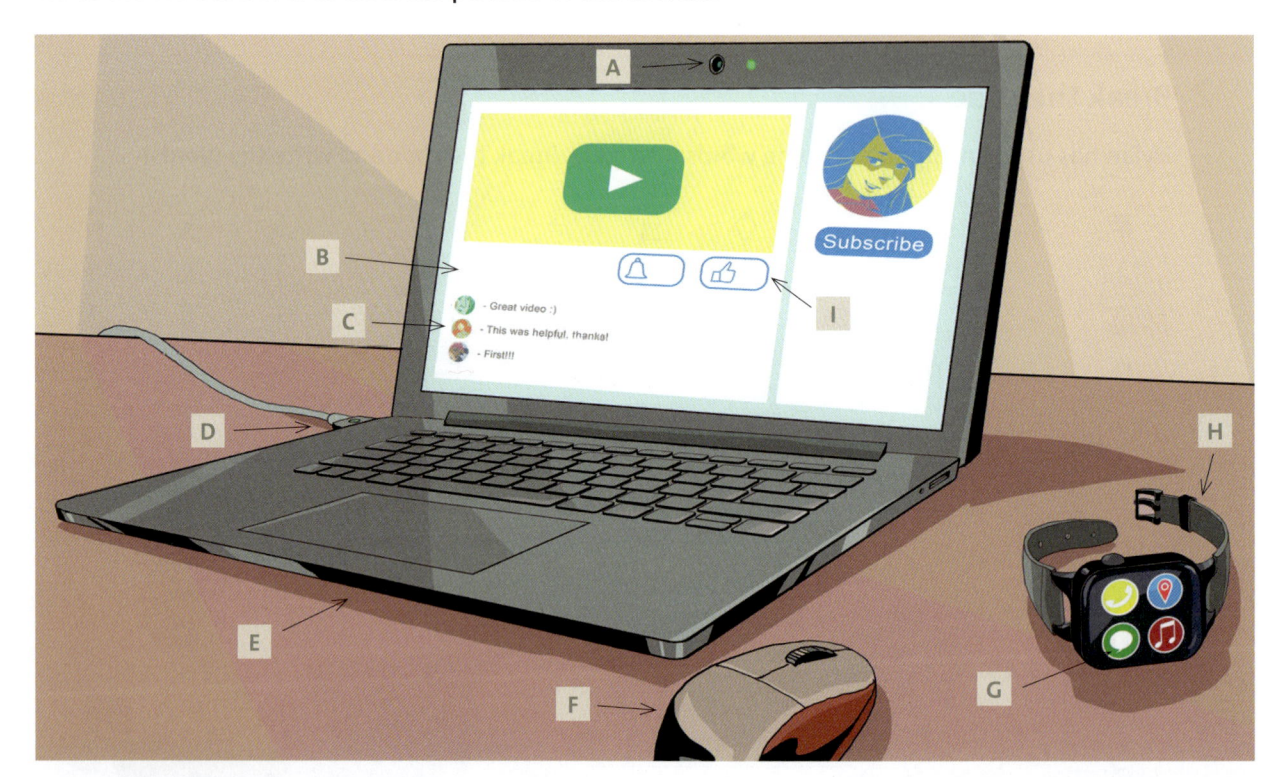

A **camera**
B **screen**
C **comment**
D **charger**
E **computer**
F **mouse**
G **app/icon**
H **smartwatch**
I **likes**

3 Categories[1]

Write the words in the box in the right categories.

choir • confused • donkey • dragon • emotional • head • jealous • neck • sheep • skin • voice

animals	singing	feelings	body
donkey	choir	emotional	neck
sheep	voice	confused	skin
dragon		jealous	head

4 Projects

Look at the instructions on the right. Write the verb 'finish' in the right form.

Sarah I've just finished my project! [finish: *present perfect*]

Liam I'm going to finish my project tomorrow. [finish: *going to-future*]

Huw Dylan is still finishing his project. [finish: *present progressive*]

Sarah Grace finished her project yesterday. [finish: *simple past*]

Liam Yes, she always finishes her work early! [finish: *simple present*]

5 Dylan's charger

Complete the conversation with the correct possessive pronouns.

Dylan Oh no, my phone is about to die[2] and I left my charger at home.
Owen, can I borrow (1) yours, please?

Owen Sorry, Dylan. I never bring (2) mine to school. Look, there's Louise.
Maybe you could borrow (3) hers?

Dylan No, she's got a different kind of charger to (4) mine. But I could ask
Promit because (5) his is the same, I think.
Hey, Promit! Do you have your charger with you? I think (6) ours are the same, right?

Promit Yeah, I do, but the Evans brothers have it because (7) theirs is broken. Sorry!

Owen Bad luck, Dylan. Looks like your phone is useless.

▶ Check

---

[1] **category** *die Kategorie* [2] **(to) die** *sterben*

Unit 5
Two Irelands: Together

1 READING The island's top 5 ▶ SB, p. 131

a) Read the website below and choose the best place for these people to visit.

1 'I want to try Irish food and learn about Irish history.' *Dublin*

2 I'm interested in buildings, especially in castles. *Cork*

3 'I want to hear Irish songs and look at beautiful paintings.' *Galway*

4 'I want to visit the coast and I love adventure!' *Carrick-a-Rede Rope Bridge*

5 'I love nature and I want to try surfing.' *Kerry*

Top 5 places to visit in Ireland and Northern Ireland

- **Galway** is a very creative city, full of art galleries and street art. You can hear traditional music in many places every night.

- **Kerry** has maybe the most beautiful road in the world, a 111-mile-long circle by the coast where you can see mountains, islands and beaches. Perfect for water sports and horse riding.

- **Cork**, the second-biggest city in Ireland, has lots of beautiful buildings. The most famous is Blarney Castle. Legend says that if you kiss[1] a stone[2] there, you will be great at speaking!

- **Dublin** is famous for being a party city with fantastic food and drink. But it also has more than 40 museums.

- **The Carrick-a-Rede Rope Bridge** is a way to walk over to a small island off the coast of Country Antrim – if you're brave! It moves a lot in the wind and it's 30 metres above the sea!

b) Which of these places would you most like to visit and why?

I'd like to visit *(Kerry* _____ *because I love hiking. / ...)*

[1] (to) **kiss** *küssen*   [2] **stone** *der Stein*

I can talk about Ireland and Northern Ireland.

Topic 1

Viewing Wordpower **5**

OPTIONAL

2 Listening A special tour of Belfast

▶ SB, p. 132

🔊 21

Listen to the tour guide and say if each sentence is true (T) or false (F).

1 This is a walking tour. **F**
2 The tour starts on Falls Road. **T**
3 All the street art in Belfast is from the 1990s. **F**
4 The tour guide remembers when there were soldiers in the city. **T**
5 All the gates in the Peace Walls are closed at night. **F**
6 The next place on the tour is a museum. **T**

3 Reading Visiting the market

▶ SB, p. 132

Read Orla's message to her friend and choose the right word for each gap.

> clothes • funny • morning • musicians • sausage • stall • world

Hey Siân! Mum, Jack and I went to St George's market this (1) _morning_ before we flew home from Belfast. It was so cool! There were 200 stalls selling everything you can think of: food, (2) _clothes_, gifts, art, everything! I bought a (3) _funny_ T-shirt to take home so I can remember this amazing trip. You can find food from all round the (4) _world_ at the market, but Jack showed us his favourite food (5) _stall_ and we got something called the Belfast Bap – it's a sandwich with (6) _sausage_, ham and egg, and it was SO good! We sat and watched some (7) _musicians_ playing the guitar while we ate. I didn't want to leave! I want to visit Belfast again soon.

Belfast Bap

5 Topic 1

OPTIONAL

4 MEDIATION A Derry B&B

▶ SB, p. 133

a) Your uncle wants to visit Derry in Northern Ireland with your cousin. He has found this advert for a B&B online, but he doesn't understand it. Read the advert and answer his questions in German.

> **Tara's Place**
>
> In the busy city centre, *Tara's Place* is perfect if you're visiting Derry! We have ten comfortable rooms on both the ground floor and first floor (5 single rooms at £55 a night, 5 large double rooms at £70 a night), all with their own modern bathroom with a bath and shower. Our beautiful rooms also have a kettle, desk and TV.
>
> There's free Wi-Fi in the dining room only.
>
> A delicious breakfast of toast, muesli and bread with tea or coffee is included[1] in the price. Visit our website now!

1 Ist das B&B außerhalb von Derry? *Nein, es ist im Stadtzentrum.*

2 Wie viel kostet ein Zimmer für zwei Personen? *Es kostet £70 pro Nacht.*

3 Welche Ausstattung haben die Zimmer? *Jedes Zimmer hat ein eigenes Badezimmer, einen Wasserkocher, Schreibtisch und Fernseher.*

4 Ich brauche ein Zimmer im Erdgeschoss – geht das? *Ja.*

5 Ich muss an einer Online-Konferenz im Zimmer teilnehmen. Gibt es WLAN? *Ja, aber nicht im Zimmer, sondern nur im Essbereich.*

6 Was gibt es zum Frühstück? *Es gibt Toast, Frühstücksflocken und Brot sowie Tee oder Kaffee.*

b) Copy the adjectives in the text which makes things in the B&B sound good.

perfect, comfortable, large, modern, beautiful, free, delicious

---

[1] **included** enthalten

I can **plan and talk about a trip.**

5 VIEWING Tell the story of the video ▶ SB, p. 134

Put the sentences in the right order. Write 1–9 in the boxes.

- [3] Tina's parents give her a cake on her birthday, but her dad doesn't have time to stay and eat some with her.
- [5] Tina 2 locks the wardrobe door and Tina can't get out.
- [9] Tina dances her new dance with the children at the dance school.
- [8] Tina's mother says she could help Tina with her dancing.
- [1] A boy talks to Tina, but she doesn't know what to say and runs away.
- [7] Tina 2 dances a very special dance. The children love it, but the dance teacher doesn't.
- [4] Tina 2 talks with the boy when Tina is too scared to talk.
- [2] Tina goes to dance practice, but has no dance partner.
- [6] Tina 2 throws Tina's mother's tablet out of the window.

6 What the words really tell us ▶ SB, p. 134

a) Read the following scene from the *Tina times two* video.

Mother & Father ((sitting at the kitchen table, showing each other pictures on their tablets))

Tina Hi. I'm going out to play. I won't go too far.

Father ((looking up from his tablet)) Don't go too far.

Mother ((looking at her tablet. She doesn't see that Tina is wearing a scarf)) Put on a scarf, love.

Tina Sure.

b) What do the words tell you about Tina's parents? Answer the questions.

1 Tina's father's words show that he _hasn't listened to Tina._

2 Tina's mother's words show that she _hasn't looked at Tina._

3 The scene shows us that Tina's parents _are more interested in their tablets than in Tina / spend more time on their tablets than on Tina._

7 What do *you* think? ▶ SB, p. 134

Do you think the story is realistic or not?

(Yes, because many parents have too little time for their children. / No, because Tina 2 isn't real.)

8 Travel words

Write the words in the box in the correct lists.

beach • bed • castle • caves • chickpeas • coach • cucumber • kettle • key • muesli • palace • plane • sausages • ship • shower • television • toast • tower • train • underground

Hotel room	Transport	Places to see	Food
bed	coach	beach	chickpeas
kettle	plane	castle	cucumber
key	ship	caves	muesli
shower	train	palace	sausages
television	underground	tower	toast

9 Limerick castle

Complete the text with the right time words.

ago • am • at (2x) • from • hour • in (3x) • pm (2x) • to • years

The Vikings came to Limerick about eleven hundred and fifty years (1) *ago* and King John built the castle that we see today three hundred and thirty (2) *years* later. It was finished (3) *in* 1210. The castle opens to visitors (4) *at* 9.30 (5) *am* every morning. (6) *From* April (7) *to* September the castle closes at 6.00 (8) *pm* and it closes one (9) *hour* earlier (11) *in* winter: at 5 (10) *pm*. There are often concerts and shows (12) *in* the evening (13) *at* weekends.

10 SPEAKING Speak English well: questions

🔊 22

a) Listen to the questions. Which go up at the end (↑) and which go down at the end (↓)?

1 Do you have a reservation?   ↑
2 How much is a double room?   ↓
3 Where are the Peace Walls?   ↓
4 Have you been to Belfast before?   ↑
5 Who is the manager of this hotel?   ↓
6 Did you have a good journey?   ↑

b) Look at your answers for a) and complete the sentence.

Yes/No-questions go *up* at the end and WH-questions go *down* at the end.

My learner log 5
OPTIONAL

In Unit 5, I was most interested in learning about *(Belfast / the Troubles / …)*

because *(I want to visit Ireland. / I'm interested in history. / …)*

My progress[1]

Complete the sentences to say how confident you are about the *I can* statements.

the easiest • quite easy • a bit difficult • the most difficult

💡 Aim for the moon, even if you land among the stars.

I can talk about Ireland and Northern Ireland. This is *(quite easy / …)* for me.

I can plan and talk about a trip. This is *(the easiest / …)* for me.

I can talk and write about Belfast. This is *(a bit difficult / …)* for me.

Looking back at this year

Look at your learner logs for all the units this year and complete the sentences.

My favourite unit was *(Unit 1 / …)* because *(I think London is a really cool city. / …)*

The easiest topic for me was *(technology / …)*

because *(lots of the words are the same in German. / …)*

The most difficult topic for me was *(the Troubles / …)*

because *(it was complicated and I don't like history. / …)*

I want to find out more about *(places in Scotland. / …)*

Next year, to improve my English, I will *(use digital help more. / listen to podcasts in English. / play my video game in English. /…)*

---

[1] **progress** *der Fortschritt*

5 Early finisher
OPTIONAL

1 A dream trip to Dublin

Read all the information and choose transport, somewhere to stay and activities for your dream trip to Dublin. You can spend a maximum of €350.

Return plane tickets to Dublin	Return train and boat to Dublin	Return coach and boat to Dublin
Two hours	Nine hours	Fifteen hours
€150	€80	€50

Central Hostel	Paddy's B&B	Hotel De Luxe
A small family room with a shared bathroom. No TV or Wi-Fi.	A family room with private bathroom and free breakfast.	A beautiful family room with private bathroom, TV with games console, fast Wi-Fi and delicious breakfast.
€40 a night	€70 a night	€100 a night

Dublin Castle	Dublin Zoo	George's Street Arcade
Explore this historical castle and its beautiful gardens and get a beautiful view of the city from the top of the tower.	See all your favourite animals, including elephants, penguins and lions in the centre of a big park.	An indoor market with great shops and food stalls.
€4	€20	free (except for what you buy!)

Bus tour	Forty Foot	National Leprechaun Museum
A bus tour of Dublin which will take you around all the main sights of the city. You can get on and off the bus to visit different places.	A local secret, this is a big cliff at the beach that is perfect for jumping into the sea and swimming – if you're brave enough to jump into cold water!	A fun museum all about the magic and legends of Ireland. You can take lots of funny photos here too!
€28	Free	€12

I'm going to travel by _(plane / …)_ because _(it's quick / …)_ _____ and stay for _(two / …)_ nights at _(the Central Hostel / …)_ because _(it's the cheapest. / …)_

I'm going to visit _(Forty Foot / …)_ and _(do a bus tour / …)_ because _(I want to see all the sights of Dublin. / …)_

But I'm not going to _(visit Dublin Zoo / …)_ because _(I don't like zoos. / …)_

▶ Check

Partner pages

Unit 1 Topic 3 | Exercise 11 ▶ WB, p. 24 ▶ SB, p. 22

Partner B: Ask your partner for the missing information and complete your menu.

How much is/are …? *What costs £ …?* *What's in a …?*

Greg's Breakfast Cafe

Big English breakfast (bacon[1], *eggs*, sausage, mushrooms[2], *baked beans*)	£7.50	Turkish breakfast (bread, hummus, cucumber, eggs, tomatoes)	£6.50
Vegetarian English breakfast (eggs, mushrooms, tomatoes, baked beans)	£6.25	Muesli with *milk* or yoghurt	£2.25
		Fruit salad	£2.75
Eggs on toast	£3.50	Tea or coffee	£1.75
Pancakes	£3.25	Fruit juice	£1.50
Toast with *butter* and jam	£2.00	Sparkling *water*	£1.50

Unit 2 Topic 1 | Exercise 4b) ▶ WB, p. 35 ▶ SB, p. 46

Look at the model from the Manchester Fashion Week. Was your drawing correct?
Then answer the questions in c) on page 35.

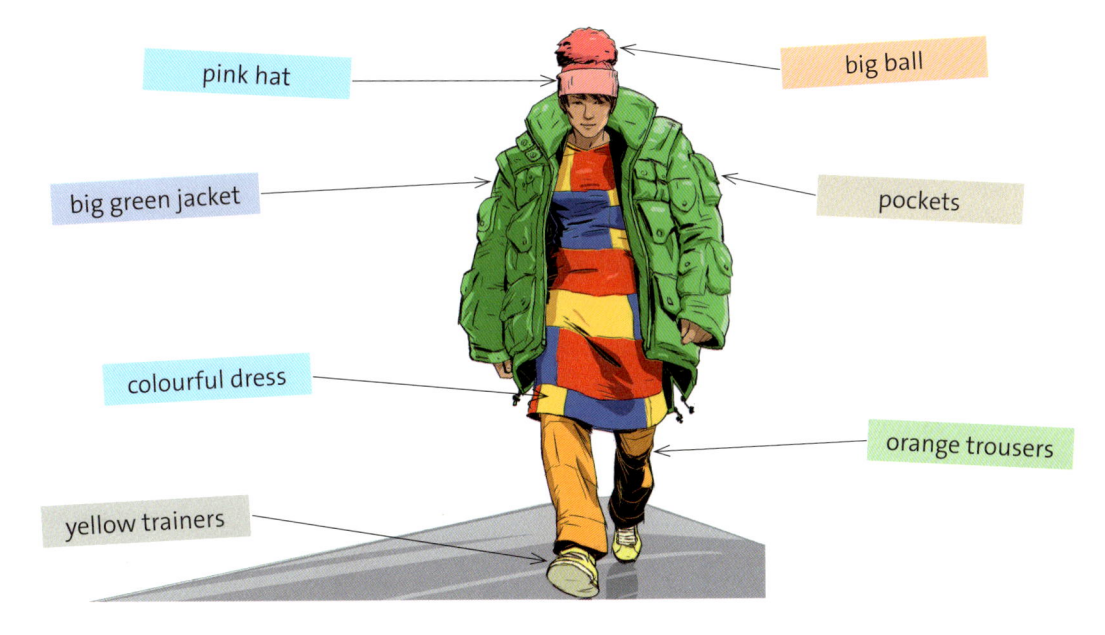

- pink hat
- big ball
- big green jacket
- pockets
- colourful dress
- orange trousers
- yellow trainers

---

[1] **bacon** *der Speck*   [2] **mushroom** *der Pilz*

Partner pages

Unit 2 Topic 3 | Exercise 13 ▶ WB, p. 42 ▶ SB, p. 54

a) Partner B: Read the advert on the right and answer your partner's questions.

CONFIDENCE CLUB

All students are welcome to come and help their confidence through different exercises. Come along to **CONFIDENCE CLUB** and you'll learn to act, dance and talk in public – and hopefully to **BELIEVE IN YOURSELF TOO**!

We meet every Thursday at lunchtime in room 7. Speak to **MRS GIBSON** to sign up!

b) Ask your partner these questions and write the answers.

1. What's your advert for? *A confidence app.*
2. How can it help people be more confident? *They can play games, watch videos or repeat compliments.*
3. When can people do this? *Any time they need it.*
4. How much does it cost? *Nothing. / It's free.*

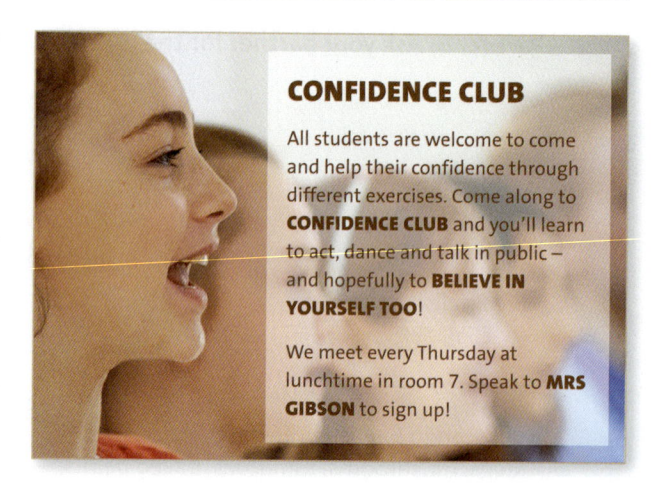

c) Which activity do you think is best and why? Write the answer and then tell your partner.

(I like the app best because you can use it any time. / I don't acting. / I like the 'confidence club' best because you can make friends. / I like dancing. / …)

Unit 3 Topic 2 | Exercise 7 ▶ WB, p. 54 ▶ SB, p. 78

a) Partner B: Answer your partner's questions and ask them for the missing information.

> How much does *skiing* cost on *Monday* at *12* o'clock?

> *Thirty* pounds.

> What can you do on *Tuesday* at *9* o'clock?

> …

	9 o'clock		12 o'clock		3 o'clock	
Monday	go-karting	£10	skiing	*£30*	swimming	£5
Tuesday	*snowboarding*	£30	*kayaking*	£15	mountain biking	*£25*
Wednesday	cliff jumping	£20	mountain biking	*£25*	*snowboarding*	£30
Thursday	swimming	*£5*	go-karting	£10	cliff jumping	£20
Friday	*kayaking*	£15	swimming	£5	*skiing*	£30

b) Decide with your partner which three activities you would both like to do. When are they and how much will it cost in total?

> I'd like to go … because it's my favourite activity.

> We can go … at … o'clock on … and at … o'clock on … It costs …

Partner pages

Unit 4 — **Topic 3 | Exercise 14** ▶ WB, p. 74 ▶ SB, p. 113

a) Your partner will explain five words. Write your partner's five words.

1 *choir*   2 *biography*   3 *Welsh people*   4 *teenager*   5 *instruction*

b) Now explain these five words to your partner in sentences with **who** or **that**.
Use **who** if possible. Don't say the word because your partner has to guess your word! ☺

1 medicine   2 Wales   3 adults   4 cyberbully   5 dragon

It's They're	an animal something people a part of Britain a person	that who	is on the flag of … you take when you … are older than … is to the west of … bullies people …

Typical tasks

Typical tasks	Häufige Arbeitsanweisungen
Act out the conversation / scene.	Führt das Gespräch / die Szene vor.
Answer the questions / partner B's questions.	Beantworte die Fragen / Partner/in Bs Fragen.
Ask questions.	Stelle Fragen.
Check with your partner.	Überprüfe mit deiner Partnerin / deinem Partner.
Choose the correct verbs / a person / ...	Wähle die richtigen Verben / eine Person / ...
Circle the right word / correct verb / ...	Kreise das richtige Wort / das richtige Verb / ... ein.
Compare the pictures / your answers / ... with a partner.	Vergleiche die Bilder / deine Antworten / ... mit einem/r Partner/in.
Complete the questions / table / ...	Vervollständige die Fragen / die Tabelle / ...
Correct the false / wrong sentences / answers.	Berichtige die falschen Sätze / Antworten.
Cross out (cross out) the numbers / wrong things / ...	Streiche die Nummern / die falschen Dinge / ... durch.
Describe the picture.	Beschreibe das Bild.
Draw pictures / lines / ...	Zeichne / Male Bilder / Linien / ...
Explain why.	Begründe (deine Antwort).
Fill the gaps with the right words.	Vervollständige die Lücken mit den richtigen Wörtern.
Find the answers / right picture / ...	Finde die Antworten / das richtige Bild / ...
Give reasons.	Begründe (deine Antwort).
Highlight the letters / words / ...	Markiere die Buchstaben / Wörter / ...
Listen again.	Höre nochmal zu.
Listen and check / read / write / ...	Höre zu und überprüfe / lies / schreibe / ...
Listen to the words / sentences / people / ...	Höre dir die Wörter / Sätze / Leute / ... an.
Look at the picture / answers / ...	Schau dir das Bild / die Antwort / ... an.
Match the pictures / ... with the sentences / ...	Ordne die Bilder / ... den Sätzen / ... zu.
Practise with a partner.	Übe mit einem/r Partner/in.
Put a cross (✘) in the box for the wrong sentences.	Setze ein Kreuzchen ins Kästchen für die falschen Sätze.
Put a tick (✓) in the box for the correct sentences / in the right boxes.	Setze ein Häkchen ins Kästchen für die richtigen Sätze / in die richtigen Kästchen.
Put the words in the right order.	Setze die Wörter in die richtige Reihenfolge.
Read about ...	Lies über ...
Read the messages / sentences / text / ...	Lies die Nachrichten / Sätze / den Text / ...
Right (✓) or wrong (✘)? / True (T) or false (F)?	Richtig oder falsch?
Swap roles.	Wechselt die Rollen.
Take turns.	Wechselt euch ab.
Talk to a partner.	Sprich mit einem/r Partner/in.
Tick the correct definition / the hobbies / ...	Hake alle richtigen Definitionen / Hobbys / ... ab.
Underline ...	Unterstreiche ...
Use the answers / letters / words / sentences / ... ... to help you.	Benutze die Antworten/ Buchstaben / Wörter / Sätze / ... ... als Hilfe.
Use words from the box.	Benutze die Wörter aus dem Kasten.
Watch part 1/2/... (again).	Sieh dir Teil 1/2/... (nochmal) an.
Write about six sports / your grandma / ...	Schreibe über sechs Sportarten / deine Oma / ...
Write the correct definitions / answers / sentences / ...	Schreibe die richtigen Definitionen / Antworten / Sätze / ...